The Meaning of The Qur'ān in Plain English

The Qur'ān
in Plain English

PART 30 WITH

Sūrat al-Fātiḥah

Iman Torres – al Haneef

THE ISLAMIC FOUNDATION

Published by
THE ISLAMIC FOUNDATION
Markfield Conference Centre,
Ratby Lane, Markfield,
Leicestershire, LE67 9SY,
United Kingdom
E-mail: publications@islamic-foundation.com
Website: www.islamic-foundation.com

Quran House, PO Box 30611, Nairobi, Kenya

PMB 3193, Kano, Nigeria

Distributed by
Kube Publishing Ltd.
Tel: +44 (01530) 249230, Fax: +44 (01530) 249656
E-mail: info@kubepublishing.com
Website: www. kubepublishing.com

British Library Cataloguing in Publication Data
A Catalogue record of this book is available from the British Library.

ISBN 978-0-86037-233-2

Typeset by: N.A. Qaddoura
Cover design by: Nasir Cadir

Printed by: IMAK Ofset, Turkey

بسم الله الرحمن الرحيم

For Muslim children everywhere

with special thanks to my teachers, husband and children
for their patience and inspiration

Contents

Introduction

The Qur'ān is the bedrock of Muslim society and the main source for fashioning Islamic life and culture. It is a book (*Kitāb*) which brought a revolution, changed societies, transformed morals and manners and imbibed people with a sense of mission and purpose in life. It is a book which is not only recited by millions of Muslims every day, in and outside the Prayer, it is a source of guidance which is reflected in the life-pattern of every Muslim in one form or another. The importance of the Qur'ān, therefore, for a Muslim is immense, not only for his or her guidance, moral and spiritual enlightenment but, most importantly, for learning how to lead a life which may bring one success in this life as well as the Next. It is quite natural that every Muslim tries his or her best to live for and by the Qur'ān, the Word of God revealed to the Last Messenger, Muḥammad ﷺ, for all times and all places.

Muslims in the West, especially the youth and children with no or little knowledge of Arabic, have for long felt the need for a simple, fluent translation of the meaning of the Qur'ān in contemporary English. It is, however, worth clarifying that no translation, however faithful and elegant, can recapture even partially the inimitable beauty and grandeur of the Arabic Qur'ān. So while efforts are being made to learn and master Arabic for studying the Qur'ān, an English translation may be used as an aid to Qur'ān study. Although many English translations of the Qur'ān are available, some of which are exceptionally good, there is not a single translation catering for the needs of the younger generation. A work designed especially for this readership has to be different from the one written for adults. What is most gratifying is that Sister Iman Torres – Al Haneef, the author of this work, being remarkably alive to the needs of young people, has produced a book which will instruct and enlighten the target audience. To begin with, she has covered the *sūrahs* of the last part (*Juz'*) *of* the Qur'ān, most of which every Muslim learns by heart at an early age and recites in daily Prayers. This will enable young readers to grasp fully what they recite and remember. I am sure, *insha' Allah* this work will go a long way in helping youth and children to gain a better understanding of the meaning and message of the Qur'ān. We hope to bring out other volumes of this work, containing translation of other *sūrahs* as and when they are ready. We look forward to suggestions and comments which may help us in improving the quality of this project.

The Islamic Foundation considers it a privilege to publish this work on the Qur'ān which, it is hoped, will meet the needs of many, in particular the younger generation born and brought up in the West. May Allah guide us to the right path and reward the author and all those who have contributed in their own way to this project (*Amīn*). I am extremely grateful to my colleagues, especially Dr. Abdur Raheem Kidwai and Brother Naiem Qaddoura, for their help in the finalization and production of the work.

Rabiʿ al-Awwal 1414
September 1993

M. Manazir Ahsan
Director General

Preface

The Qur'ān is the final scripture of the One God, Allah, to all humanity. It was revealed in the Arabic language as a completion of all previous scriptures, from God through the Angel Jibra'īl (Gabriel) عليه السلام to the Prophet Muḥammad ﷺ in the seventh century of the Christian Era, over a period of 23 years. It contains guidance for all aspects of human life, and its words are as fresh and relevant today as when they were first sent down.

Arabic is a very precise language and the meanings of its words are more concise and subtle than many other languages; this is one of the reasons it is said that the Qur'ān cannot really be translated. Also, the classical Arabic of the Qur'ān is very poetic and inspiring; many of its verses rhyme, and there is no way to imitate this lovely sound in English. Therefore, it is understood that the best way to study the Qur'ān is to learn the classical Arabic language in which it was revealed under the guidance of a teacher, and the best way to read it is to recite it out loud according to the rules of *tajwīd* (proper recitation) in a beautiful voice. However, there are not yet enough teachers of the Qur'ān and Arabic in the English-speaking world to make this possible for everyone, and not everyone has the same ability to learn language. There are already many translations of the Qur'ān available in English, but the most widely-used are written in formal 'Shakespearian' English which not many young people today understand, with a vocabulary which can even be unclear to many adults.

Foreign-born parents and teachers find it difficult to explain the Qur'ān's meanings to their children who may speak only English. Adult converts to Islam who speak languages in which a good Qur'ān translation does not yet exist are learning English in increasing numbers, but may have trouble with complex sentences and archaic vocabulary.

Therefore, I am offering this simple translation in the hope that it will be inviting and practical; that it will make the words of Allah accessible to more people, young and old, in and out of the classroom. I have begun with the last thirtieth part, because the vast majority of Muslims begin to memorize these *sūrahs* before going on to study others. Also included in this work is the translation of the opening *sūrah* of the Qur'ān, *al-Fātiḥah,* which is recited in every *Ṣalāt* (Prayer). If Allah wills, more parts may be completed in the future. The text has been reviewed for accuracy by experts, but I ask Allah's forgiveness for any errors which may remain, as well as the reader's tolerance. May Allah grant us the love and remembrance of His Holy Book and the strength to follow His beloved Prophet Muḥammad ﷺ, the 'walking example of the Qur'ān', so that its eternal message will bear fruit in our daily lives. *Amīn.*

Iman Torres – Al Haneef

Notes

- This English translation has been kept as simple as possible so that it can be understood by children as young as seven with occasional reference to a dictionary. However, more advanced vocabulary has been used in the notes, which should be manageable for children from the age of 10+.
- Words contained in parentheses ( ) do not specifically exist in the Arabic text but are to be understood as an integral part of the meaning of the *āyah.*
- The Library of Congress system has been used for transliteration, except that al- is changed to ad-, ar-, etc. before the "sun letters". Definitions for important or frequently-occurring Arabic vocabulary words (in italics in the text) are provided in a glossary at the end of the book.
- The following calligraphic symboles have been used to indicate respect:

ﷺ	(peace and blessings be upon him) when mentioning the Prophet Muḥammad
عليه السلام	(on him be peace) for any other Prophet. and the angel Jibrā'īl
رضي الله عنه and رضي الله عنهم	(may Allah be pleased with him/them) for the Prophet's Companions.

The Etiquette of Reading and Studying the Qur'ān

The Qur'ān is Allah's holy word to humanity. Whoever wishes to read, recite or study the Qur'ān should do so according to the rules of proper *adab*, or etiquette, so that he may earn Allah's pleasure and have his efforts rewarded.

In between readings, we should:

- Always keep the Qur'ān clean, in a high and honoured place.

When reading, reciting or studying the Qur'ān, we should keep the conditions of ṣalāh*:*

- Make *wuḍū'* before touching it or reading from it.[1]
- Make the intention to read or study for Allah's pleasure before beginning. Imagine that we are sitting in front of Allah and He is listening.
- Face the *qiblah* dressed as we would for prayer, sitting in a clean place in a humble and respectful posture.

---

1. A person without *wuḍū'* may recite the Qur'ān from memory, but should not touch a copy of the text. Menstruating girls and women should not touch the text unless (according to some scholars) they are following a course of study.

2. Meaning, 'I seek Allah's protection from the cursed Satan', 'In the name of Allah, the All-Merciful, Most Kind'.

- Begin with *a'ūdhu bi-llāhi minash-shayṭānir-rajīm, bismillāhir-raḥmānir-raḥīm.*[2]
- Read clearly, with good pronunciation in a beautiful tone of voice.
- Say *Ṣadaqal-Lāhul 'aẓīm*[3] when we finish the reading, and make a *du'ā'* asking Allah to accept it.

We should also try to:

- Read some of the Qur'ān every day, preferably at a regular time.
- Learn the rules of correct recitation (*tajwīd*) in order to avoid pronouncing words incorrectly, or accidentally saying another word which would change the meaning.[4]
- Learn the classical Arabic language of the Qur'ān, in order to understand it better.
- Do our best to try to think about what we have read, and put it into practice.
- Memorize as many *sūrahs* as we can.

---

3. Meaning, 'Allah, the Great One spoke the truth'.

4. There are many ways to learn tajwid if one doesn't have a teacher nearby: online courses or websites, computer software, or books with CDs or audiocassettes showing the right pronunciation.

Transliteration

Guide to Pronouncing Arabic Words

Some Arabic vowels and sounds have no English equivalent. In order to help readers overcome this problem some special marks have been put on certain words in this book.

For example, ā, ī and ū stand for the vowel sounds aa (as in path), ee (as in feet) and oo (as in pool) respectively.

Similarly, the signs (ʼ) and (ʻ) have been used for the Arabic letters 'hamza' (as in *Wuḍūʼ*) and ʻayn (as in *Kaʻbah*).

Arabic Alphabet and its English Equivalent

ʼ	ء	d	د	ḍ	ض	k	ك
b	ب	dh	ذ	ṭ	ط	l	ل
t	ت	r	ر	ẓ	ظ	m	م
th	ث	z	ز	ʻ	ع	n	ن
j	ج	s	س	gh	غ	h	هـ
ḥ	ح	sh	ش	f	ف	w	و
kh	خ	ṣ	ص	q	ق	y	ي

1

al-Fātiḥah [The Opening]

MAKKAN PERIOD

Sūrat al-Fātiḥah is very special for many reasons. It is the beautiful opening of the Book of Allah. It is called by many names: *Umm al-Kitāb* (Mother of the Book), *al-Ḥamd* (the Praise), *as-Sab' al-Mathānī* (the Seven Oft-Repeated Verses – because it is repeated in *ṣalāh), ash-Shifā'* (the Sūrah of Healing), *al-Kāfiyah* (the Sufficient One), and *al-Asās* (the Foundation).

Unlike the other *sūrahs* which were revealed only once, it is reported that *Sūrat al-Fātiḥah* was revealed twice: once in Makkah and once in Madīnah. An angel once told the Prophet ﷺ that it is a light which has never been given to any other prophet before him. It is the main *du'ā'* of the Muslims, and we must recite it in every *rak'ah* of *ṣalāh.* Because of this, it is the most often-repeated prayer in the world: many millions of Muslims all over the world recite it at least 17 times a day.

Placed at the beginning of the Qur'ān, this *sūrah* is actually a prayer. Allah asks us to read the Qur'ān with the aim of finding out 'the straight path' and true guidance. This *sūrah* is thus a human prayer and the rest of the Qur'ān is Allah's response, showing us 'the Straight Path' which will bring us success in both this life and the Next. It is divided into two parts. In the first part, He shows us how we should speak *about* Him: He is kind, merciful, and good to us, and deserves all of our praise. He is our Master and King. We will stand before Him on the Day of Judgement with our actions, good and bad.

In the second part, He teaches us how to speak *to* Him; we address Allah Who is the only One we worship and ask for help, and we ask Him to guide us both in this life and the Next. We ask Allah to keep us doing the things which He is pleased with, and not the ones which make Him angry, or will lead to us becoming confused and lost.

Al-Fātiḥah

سُورَةُ الفَاتِحَةِ

[The Opening]

[1] *In the name of Allah, the All-Merciful, the Most Kind*

بِسْمِ ٱللَّهِ ٱلرَّحْمَٰنِ ٱلرَّحِيمِ ﴿١﴾

[2] Praise is for Allah, Master of the Universe,

ٱلْحَمْدُ لِلَّهِ رَبِّ ٱلْعَٰلَمِينَ ﴿٢﴾

[3] the All-Merciful, the Most Kind,

ٱلرَّحْمَٰنِ ٱلرَّحِيمِ ﴿٣﴾

[4] King[5] of the Day of Judgement.

مَٰلِكِ يَوْمِ ٱلدِّينِ ﴿٤﴾

[5] You are the One we worship (O Allah); You are the One we ask for help.

إِيَّاكَ نَعْبُدُ وَإِيَّاكَ نَسْتَعِينُ ﴿٥﴾

[6] Show us the Straight Path;

ٱهْدِنَا ٱلصِّرَٰطَ ٱلْمُسْتَقِيمَ ﴿٦﴾

[7] the Path of those whom You are pleased with – not the path of those who deserve Your anger, nor of those who become lost.

صِرَٰطَ ٱلَّذِينَ أَنْعَمْتَ عَلَيْهِمْ غَيْرِ
ٱلْمَغْضُوبِ عَلَيْهِمْ وَلَا ٱلضَّآلِّينَ ﴿٧﴾

---

5. Or Master.

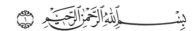

78

an-Naba' [The Awesome News]

MAKKAN PERIOD

This is one of the earliest Makkan *sūrahs,* out of a series whose theme is the Resurrection, Judgement and life after death. When the Prophet Muḥammad ﷺ first began to preach his message in Makkah, it was very simple: there is only One God, I am His Prophet, and everyone will be raised from death for a final Judgement, after which they will be rewarded or punished for their deeds on earth.

The Makkans found the first two parts of the message more reasonable than the last. Although they worshipped many 'gods', they believed that Allah was the greatest of these gods. They also accepted that the Prophet Muḥammad ﷺ was an honest and sincere person, known throughout his life for his wisdom and trustworthiness. Such a person would not be expected to lie for his own benefit (this was, in fact, one of the reasons that some people suggested that perhaps the Prophet ﷺ was possessed by a *jinn,* since he was clearly not a liar). But the idea of a final Resurrection Day was something they had never heard of before, and most of the people found it unacceptable. 'How could dry bones come alive again?', they said.

This *sūrah* and the others which follow therefore draw attention to Allah's Power –

it is He Who created so many wonders in the world, so much beauty! Isn't the One Who gave everything its first life also able to bring everything back to life a second time? Secondly, the *sūrah* focuses on the meaning behind all of this wonderful creation. Look around you! See the earth with its firm mountains, grain, vegetables, and plentiful rain, the heavens above with the blazing sun, the changing of night and day which allows us to work in light and rest in dark. Is it possible in a world in which everything has been made so perfectly, with so much care, that the whole purpose of life is simply to eat, drink, sleep, work, marry, grow old and die? No. This life is rather a test; those who pass it will be richly rewarded, and those who fail will regret it bitterly. They will suddenly realize that they have wasted their most sacred possession – life itself – and will wish at that moment that they could turn into dust to escape that sense of failure and the doom of punishment.

an-Naba'

سُورَةُ النَّبَإِ

[The Awesome News]

In the name of Allah, the All-Merciful, the Most Kind

بِسْمِ ٱللَّهِ ٱلرَّحْمَٰنِ ٱلرَّحِيمِ

[1] What do they question each other about?

عَمَّ يَتَسَآءَلُونَ ١

[2] About the awesome news

عَنِ ٱلنَّبَإِ ٱلْعَظِيمِ ٢

[3] which they cannot agree on.[6]

ٱلَّذِى هُمْ فِيهِ مُخْتَلِفُونَ ٣

[4] No! But they will come to know (soon enough).

كَلَّا سَيَعْلَمُونَ ٤

[5] No! Surely they will find out!

ثُمَّ كَلَّا سَيَعْلَمُونَ ٥

[6] Have We not made the earth easy and wide[7]

أَلَمْ نَجْعَلِ ٱلْأَرْضَ مِهَٰدًا ٦

---

6. The awesome news which they could not agree upon was the news of the Resurrection and life after death.

7. *Mihādā* means to prepare a place to make it easy to use, such as in laying a road or smoothing an area.

[7] and (We made) the mountains as pegs (to hold it firm),

وَٱلْجِبَالَ أَوْتَادًا ﴿٧﴾

[8] and created you in pairs,[8]

وَخَلَقْنَٰكُمْ أَزْوَٰجًا ﴿٨﴾

[9] and have made your sleep for rest,

وَجَعَلْنَا نَوْمَكُمْ سُبَاتًا ﴿٩﴾

[10] and have made the night as a cloak,[9]

وَجَعَلْنَا ٱلَّيْلَ لِبَاسًا ﴿١٠﴾

[11] and have made the day as a time to earn your living?[10]

وَجَعَلْنَا ٱلنَّهَارَ مَعَاشًا ﴿١١﴾

[12] And We have built above you seven strong heavens,

وَبَنَيْنَا فَوْقَكُمْ سَبْعًا شِدَادًا ﴿١٢﴾

[13] and have made a blazing lamp,[11]

وَجَعَلْنَا سِرَاجًا وَهَّاجًا ﴿١٣﴾

---

8. Allah created many animals and plants in pairs of male and female.

9. *Libāsā* means to dress or cover; night covers everything with darkness like a cloak or cape.

10. *Maʿāshā* means every kind of activity or work needed to maintain life.

11. The sun.

[14] and have sent down from the rain clouds abundant water,

وَأَنزَلۡنَا مِنَ ٱلۡمُعۡصِرَٰتِ مَآءٗ
ثَجَّاجٗا ١٤

[15] so that We may produce with it grain and vegetables,

لِّنُخۡرِجَ بِهِۦ حَبّٗا وَنَبَاتٗا ١٥

[16] and gardens, thick with leaves.

وَجَنَّٰتٍ أَلۡفَافًا ١٦

[17] Surely the Day of Decision has a set time;

إِنَّ يَوۡمَ ٱلۡفَصۡلِ كَانَ مِيقَٰتٗا ١٧

[18] a Day when the trumpet will be blown, and you shall come in great crowds

يَوۡمَ يُنفَخُ فِي ٱلصُّورِ فَتَأۡتُونَ
أَفۡوَاجٗا ١٨

[19] and the heaven will be opened as if there were gates (in it),

وَفُتِحَتِ ٱلسَّمَآءُ فَكَانَتۡ أَبۡوَٰبٗا ١٩

[20] and the mountains shall vanish as if they were a mirage.

وَسُيِّرَتِ ٱلۡجِبَالُ فَكَانَتۡ سَرَابًا ٢٠

[21] Surely Hell is waiting in ambush,

إِنَّ جَهَنَّمَ كَانَتۡ مِرۡصَادٗا ٢١

[22] a home for those who pass the limits,

لِّلطَّٰغِينَ مَـَٔابًا ﴿٢٢﴾

[23] living there for ages,

لَّٰبِثِينَ فِيهَآ أَحْقَابًا ﴿٢٣﴾

[24] tasting no coolness there, nor any drink

لَّا يَذُوقُونَ فِيهَا بَرْدًا وَلَا شَرَابًا ﴿٢٤﴾

[25] except boiling water and filthy fluids:[12]

إِلَّا حَمِيمًا وَغَسَّاقًا ﴿٢٥﴾

[26] a punishment to fit the crime.

جَزَآءً وِفَاقًا ﴿٢٦﴾

[27] Look, they did not think that their deeds would be counted,

إِنَّهُمْ كَانُوا۟ لَا يَرْجُونَ حِسَابًا ﴿٢٧﴾

[28] but they called Our verses lies and denied them;

وَكَذَّبُوا۟ بِـَٔايَٰتِنَا كِذَّابًا ﴿٢٨﴾

[29] and We have recorded everything in a Book.

وَكُلَّ شَىْءٍ أَحْصَيْنَٰهُ كِتَٰبًا ﴿٢٩﴾

---

12. Filthy fluids – such as the sweat, tears, and pus of the people of Hell.

[30] So taste (what you have earned). We will not give you more of anything except punishment.

فَذُوقُوا۟ فَلَن نَّزِيدَكُمْ إِلَّا عَذَابًا ٣٠

[31] Truly, for the righteous ones there will be a place of victory –

إِنَّ لِلْمُتَّقِينَ مَفَازًا ٣١

[32] private gardens and grapevines,

حَدَآئِقَ وَأَعْنَٰبًا ٣٢

[33] and young women, the same age (as them, for company),

وَكَوَاعِبَ أَتْرَابًا ٣٣

[34] and a cup, full (to the brim).

وَكَأْسًا دِهَاقًا ٣٤

[35] There, they never hear trivial talk[13] or lies –

لَّا يَسْمَعُونَ فِيهَا لَغْوًا وَلَا كِذَّٰبًا ٣٥

[36] a reward from your Lord; a satisfying gift

جَزَآءً مِّن رَّبِّكَ عَطَآءً حِسَابًا ٣٦

---

13. Trivial talk – useless, vain, idle talk; speaking of things which are not important. The drink given to the people of Paradise will not make them drunk, and no foolish words will be spoken there.

[37] (from) the Lord of the heavens and the earth and all that is between them, the All-Merciful, with Whom no one has the power to argue.

رَّبِّ ٱلسَّمَٰوَٰتِ وَٱلْأَرْضِ
وَمَا بَيْنَهُمَا ٱلرَّحْمَٰنِ ۖ لَا يَمْلِكُونَ
مِنْهُ خِطَابًا ٣٧

[38] On the day the Spirit[14] and the angels stand in rows, no one will speak except he who has the permission of the All-Merciful, and who says what is right.

يَوْمَ يَقُومُ ٱلرُّوحُ وَٱلْمَلَٰٓئِكَةُ صَفًّا ۖ
لَّا يَتَكَلَّمُونَ إِلَّا مَنْ أَذِنَ لَهُ
ٱلرَّحْمَٰنُ وَقَالَ صَوَابًا ٣٨

[39] That is the Day of Truth; so whoever wishes should find a way to return to his Lord![15]

ذَٰلِكَ ٱلْيَوْمُ ٱلْحَقُّ ۖ فَمَن شَآءَ ٱتَّخَذَ
إِلَىٰ رَبِّهِۦ مَـَٔابًا ٣٩

[40] Truly, We have warned you about a nearby punishment, on a Day when a man will see (the deeds) that his own hands have sent before him, and the unbeliever will cry, 'Oh, if only I were dust!'

إِنَّآ أَنذَرْنَٰكُمْ عَذَابًا قَرِيبًا يَوْمَ
يَنظُرُ ٱلْمَرْءُ مَا قَدَّمَتْ يَدَاهُ وَيَقُولُ
ٱلْكَافِرُ يَٰلَيْتَنِى كُنتُ تُرَٰبًۢا ٤٠

---

14. Qur'ānic scholars believe that 'the Spirit' means the Angel Jibrā'īl عليه السلام, or other great angels who are very close to Allah, or possibly the spirits of men lined up in ranks.

15. 'Return to his Lord', meaning through obedience to Allah's commands, which will save one from punishment.

79

an-Nāzi'āt [Those who Pull Out]

MAKKAN PERIOD

This *sūrah* is another in the series whose theme is Resurrection and Judgement. It takes its name from an oath in the first verse which, according to most Qur'ānic scholars, refers to angels. There are angels who have the job of pulling out the souls of the unbelievers in a rough way at the moment of death, those who gently pull out the souls of the believers, and those who have various other tasks which they rush to fulfil in carrying out Allah's commands.[16]

Why does the *sūrah* begin by speaking of angels? The Makkans already believed in the existence of angels (although they mistakenly worshipped them as daughters of Allah); they agreed that angels took out the souls of people at the time of death. The Qur'ān speaks to these people, saying: if you believe that the angels take out the souls by God's command, why not accept that these same angels can return the souls to their resurrected bodies? If you believe that angels carry out Allah's orders throughout the universe by bringing rain clouds, guiding the movements of the stars and so forth, why not accept that they can also bring about changes in this creation, such

16. Other scholars believe that the verses refer to stars and planets.

as the great earthquake on the Last Day?

The middle section of *an-Nāziʿāt* mentions part of the story of the Prophet Mūsā عليه السلام as a lesson and warning for those who disbelieve. The Prophet Mūsā عليه السلام invited the wicked Pharaoh in polite and easy terms to accept Islam, but he refused and remained arrogant. He and his people were punished by many plagues for their stubbornly bad behaviour. Finally, the Pharaoh and his men were drowned while chasing the believers who were being led by Mūsā عليه السلام out of Egypt. Although he was one of the most powerful kings in the world, he could not escape his well-deserved punishment.[17]

The last part of the *sūrah* speaks of 'the day when people will remember all of the things they were trying to achieve', saying that when people awaken to the Judgement, 'it will seem as if they had only lived for an evening, or (at most) until the next morning'. Many people who have had near-death experiences, such as by drowning, or in car accidents, say that when they felt they were going to die, they suddenly saw pictures of their whole life flashing before their eyes like a film or video-tape being fast-forwarded. At that moment time became 'stretched', so that they saw so many events in their lives in just a few seconds. Allah says that, time will be altered for people on Judgement Day. It will seem as though our entire lives lasted no more than a day.

---

17. The full story of Mūsā عليه السلام and Pharaoh is told in many other places in the Qurʾān: *al-Baqarah* 2:49-71, *al-Aʿrāf* 7: 103-41, *Yūnus* 10: 75-92, *Ṭā Hā* 20: 9-79, *al-Qaṣaṣ* 28: 3-46, *Ghāfir* 40: 23-45 and *az-Zukhruf* 43: 46-56.

an-Nāzi'āt

[Those who Pull Out]

سُورَةُ النَّازِعَاتِ

In the name of Allah, the All-Merciful, the Most Kind

بِسْمِ ٱللَّهِ ٱلرَّحْمَـٰنِ ٱلرَّحِيمِ

[1] By those who pull out harshly,[18]

وَٱلنَّـٰزِعَـٰتِ غَرْقًا ١

[2] by those who draw out gently,

وَٱلنَّـٰشِطَـٰتِ نَشْطًا ٢

[3] by those who float along,

وَٱلسَّـٰبِحَـٰتِ سَبْحًا ٣

[4] by those who hurry forward,

فَٱلسَّـٰبِقَـٰتِ سَبْقًا ٤

[5] and by those who manage the affairs (of their Lord)!

فَٱلْمُدَبِّرَٰتِ أَمْرًا ٥

[6] On the Day when the (first) earthquake[19] (violently) shakes everything,

يَوْمَ تَرْجُفُ ٱلرَّاجِفَةُ ٦

---

18. The Angel of Death, 'Azra'īl عليه السلام, is in charge of taking out the soul of each person when he dies, and he has other angels to help carry out Allah's commands. He is one of the four archangels, or chief angels.

19. This may mean the blast of the trumpet sounded by the Angel Isrāfīl عليه السلام on the Last Day which will cause every living being to die.

[7] and the aftershock follows it,[20]

تَتۡبَعُهَا ٱلرَّادِفَةُ ٧

[8] on that Day hearts will be pounding,

قُلُوبٞ يَوۡمَئِذٖ وَاجِفَةٌ ٨

[9] and their eyes will be cast down.

أَبۡصَٰرُهَا خَٰشِعَةٞ ٩

[10] (Now) they say, 'Shall we really be returned to the way we were before,

يَقُولُونَ أَءِنَّا لَمَرۡدُودُونَ فِي
ٱلۡحَافِرَةِ ١٠

[11] even after we are crumbled bones?'

أَءِذَا كُنَّا عِظَٰمٗا نَّخِرَةٗ ١١

[12] They say, 'Then that would be a return with loss.'

قَالُواْ تِلۡكَ إِذٗا كَرَّةٌ خَاسِرَةٞ ١٢

[13] But it will only be a single Shout[21]

فَإِنَّمَا هِيَ زَجۡرَةٞ وَٰحِدَةٞ ١٣

---

20. This refers to the second blowing of the trumpet which will wake all the dead. (For details see *Sūrah az-Zumar* 39: 68.)

21. A single shout of an angel, or the blast of the trumpet at the beginning of the Resurrection.

[14] and they shall awaken to be gathered on the open plain.[22]

فَإِذَا هُم بِٱلسَّاهِرَةِ ١٤

[15] Has the story of Mūsā reached you?

هَلۡ أَتَىٰكَ حَدِيثُ مُوسَىٰٓ ١٥

[16] When his Lord called him in the holy valley of Ṭuwā, (saying)

إِذۡ نَادَىٰهُ رَبُّهُۥ بِٱلۡوَادِ ٱلۡمُقَدَّسِ طُوًى ١٦

[17] 'Go to Pharaoh, for he has truly crossed his limit.

ٱذۡهَبۡ إِلَىٰ فِرۡعَوۡنَ إِنَّهُۥ طَغَىٰ ١٧

[18] And say to him, "Would you like to be purified?"

فَقُلۡ هَل لَّكَ إِلَىٰٓ أَن تَزَكَّىٰ ١٨

[19] "And shall I guide you to your Lord, so that you will be in awe of Him?"

وَأَهۡدِيَكَ إِلَىٰ رَبِّكَ فَتَخۡشَىٰ ١٩

[20] And he (Mūsā) showed him the great[23] sign.

فَأَرَىٰهُ ٱلۡأٓيَةَ ٱلۡكُبۡرَىٰ ٢٠

---

22. The Arabic word *sāhira* has two meanings: 'to awaken' and 'the flat earth'. During the Resurrection, people will be suddenly 'woken up' for the Judgement, for which they will be assembled on a great, open plain.

23. Some scholars say that the great sign was the hand of the Prophet Mūsā عليه السلام which became shining white when he put it into his shirt. Others say that it was his walking stick, which turned into a snake and ate the other snakes of Pharaoh's magicians.

[21] But he (Pharaoh) rejected it and disobeyed,

فَكَذَّبَ وَعَصَىٰ ٢١

[22] and he turned his back, hurrying (to do mischief),

ثُمَّ أَدْبَرَ يَسْعَىٰ ٢٢

[23] then he gathered (his people) and proclaimed:

فَحَشَرَ فَنَادَىٰ ٢٣

[24] 'I, (Pharaoh), am your Lord, the Most High!'[24]

فَقَالَ أَنَا رَبُّكُمُ ٱلْأَعْلَىٰ ٢٤

[25] So Allah seized him with the punishment of the Next Life as well as this one.

فَأَخَذَهُ ٱللَّهُ نَكَالَ ٱلْآخِرَةِ
وَٱلْأُولَىٰ ٢٥

[26] Surely this is a lesson for one who fears (Allah).

إِنَّ فِي ذَٰلِكَ لَعِبْرَةً لِّمَن يَخْشَىٰ ٢٦

[27] What, are you harder to create than the heaven that Allah made?

ءَأَنتُمْ أَشَدُّ خَلْقًا أَمِ ٱلسَّمَآءُ بَنَىٰهَا ٢٧

---

24. The ancient Egyptians worshipped many idols in the form of animals and mythological creatures, and they believed that their ruler, the Pharaoh, was a living god. Some scholars believe that Ramses II was the Pharaoh of Moses' time, and that when he was drowned in the Red Sea his body was saved and preserved. The body of Ramses II was discovered by archeologists and has been shown in exhibitions throughout the world. He was a very arrogant king who spent much of the public treasury on making huge statues of himself and various works showing his conquests and achievements.

[28] He raised the height of it, and put it in perfect order,

رَفَعَ سَمْكَهَا فَسَوَّىٰهَا ﴿٢٨﴾

[29] and darkened its night, and brought out its bright light.

وَأَغْطَشَ لَيْلَهَا وَأَخْرَجَ ضُحَىٰهَا ﴿٢٩﴾

[30] And the earth – after that He spread it out,

وَٱلْأَرْضَ بَعْدَ ذَٰلِكَ دَحَىٰهَآ ﴿٣٠﴾

[31] and drew out from it its water and its pastures,

أَخْرَجَ مِنْهَا مَآءَهَا وَمَرْعَىٰهَا ﴿٣١﴾

[32] and He set the mountains firm –

وَٱلْجِبَالَ أَرْسَىٰهَا ﴿٣٢﴾

[33] for the comfort of you and your flocks.

مَتَٰعًا لَّكُمْ وَلِأَنْعَٰمِكُمْ ﴿٣٣﴾

[34] But when the great disaster comes,

فَإِذَا جَآءَتِ ٱلطَّآمَّةُ ٱلْكُبْرَىٰ ﴿٣٤﴾

[35] the day when people will remember all of the things they were trying to achieve

يَوْمَ يَتَذَكَّرُ ٱلْإِنسَٰنُ مَا سَعَىٰ ﴿٣٥﴾

[36] and Hell will be in full view for all to see;

وَبُرِّزَتِ ٱلْجَحِيمُ لِمَن يَرَىٰ ﴿٣٦﴾

[37] then, as for the one who was rebellious

فَأَمَّا مَن طَغَىٰ ﴿٣٧﴾

[38] and chose the life of this world,

وَءَاثَرَ ٱلْحَيَوٰةَ ٱلدُّنْيَا ﴿٣٨﴾

[39] surely Hell will be his home.

فَإِنَّ ٱلْجَحِيمَ هِىَ ٱلْمَأْوَىٰ ﴿٣٩﴾

[40] But as for the one who was afraid to stand before Allah (for the Judgement) and kept himself from lower desires,[25]

وَأَمَّا مَنْ خَافَ مَقَامَ رَبِّهِۦ وَنَهَى
ٱلنَّفْسَ عَنِ ٱلْهَوَىٰ ﴿٤٠﴾

[41] surely the Garden will be his home.

فَإِنَّ ٱلْجَنَّةَ هِىَ ٱلْمَأْوَىٰ ﴿٤١﴾

[42] They ask you about the Hour: 'When will it come?'

يَسْـَٔلُونَكَ عَنِ ٱلسَّاعَةِ أَيَّانَ
مُرْسَىٰهَا ﴿٤٢﴾

[43] Why are you mentioning it?

فِيمَ أَنتَ مِن ذِكْرَىٰهَآ ﴿٤٣﴾

---

25. Everyone desires certain things which are *ḥalāl* and necessary – like food, drink, love, money, friends and acceptance. When these desires are fulfilled outside the limits which Allah has set or beyond the guidelines of the Prophet ﷺ, they become destructive and are called 'lower desires'.

[44] Your Lord alone knows the final end of it.[26]

إِلَىٰ رَبِّكَ مُنتَهَىٰهَآ ﴿٤٤﴾

[45] You are only a warner to those who fear it.

إِنَّمَآ أَنتَ مُنذِرُ مَن يَخۡشَىٰهَا ﴿٤٥﴾

[46] On the Day that they see it, it will seem as if they had only lived for an evening, or (at the most) until the next morning!

كَأَنَّهُمۡ يَوۡمَ يَرَوۡنَهَا لَمۡ يَلۡبَثُوٓاْ
إِلَّا عَشِيَّةً أَوۡ ضُحَىٰهَا ﴿٤٦﴾

---

26. Allah is the only One Who knows exactly when the Day of Resurrection will come, although He told the Prophet Muḥammad ﷺ signs of its coming.

80

'Abasa [He Frowned]

MAKKAN PERIOD

According to most scholars, this *sūrah* is one of the few places in the Qur'ān in which Allah corrects the Prophet Muḥammad ﷺ for a minor, unintentional mistake.[27] This is the story behind it. The Prophet ﷺ had been busy inviting the leaders of the Quraysh to accept Islam. He knew that if more powerful and influential people became Muslims it would help to establish Islam in Makkah. At that time, the rich and powerful unbelievers were persecuting the early Muslims in many ways, making their lives very difficult. The beloved Prophet ﷺ was in the middle of a conversation with one of them when a poor, blind Muslim named 'Abdullāh bin Umm Maktūm ؓ interrupted him, to ask about the Qur'ān. The Prophet ﷺ did not want to be disturbed at that moment so he waited before replying, and the blind man's feelings might have been hurt. Then the other man frowned at the poor, blind man standing near him, and left without accepting Islam.

Allah revealed this *sūrah* after this event, and it is one of the places in the Qur'ān

27. Prophets can make mistakes – so-called 'human errors' – but are protected from committing sins so that they can serve as models of excellent behaviour for others to follow.

which is quoted by Muslims to unbelievers who claim that the Prophet ﷺ wrote the Qur'ān himself. If the Prophet ﷺ wrote it for his own benefit – *astaghfirullāh* (Allah forbid that we should believe that) – then why would he make himself look less than perfect in it?

Actually, the Prophet ﷺ was not in the habit of favouring the rich and powerful over the poor or disabled at all. He was a great friend of the poor and lived a very poor and humble lifestyle himself, always preferring to give to others rather than to keep for himself. But he took special notice of 'Abdullāh the blind man after that, and honoured him, saying, 'Welcome to the man on whose behalf my Lord has corrected me' – or, for his sake, Allah disciplined me. 'Abdullāh bin Umm Maktūm ؓ was one of the earliest Muslims and did whatever was within his ability to help in the way of Allah.

The other part of this *sūrah* (verses 17-42) is addressed to unbelievers, criticizing them for their lack of gratitute and failure to recognize the One True God, despite His abundant generosity. It is followed by a graphic, awesome account of the Last Day when everyone will be so worried about his own fate that he will run from his own mother, father, wife, children and brother.

'Abasa

[He Frowned]

سُورَةُ عَبَسَ

In the name of Allah, the All-Merciful, the Most Kind

بِسْمِ ٱللَّهِ ٱلرَّحْمَٰنِ ٱلرَّحِيمِ

[1] He frowned and turned away

عَبَسَ وَتَوَلَّىٰٓ ١

[2] because the blind man came to him (interrupting).

أَن جَآءَهُ ٱلْأَعْمَىٰ ٢

[3] And how would you know? – maybe he would grow in purity

وَمَا يُدْرِيكَ لَعَلَّهُۥ يَزَّكَّىٰٓ ٣

[4] or be reminded, and the reminder would help him!

أَوْ يَذَّكَّرُ فَتَنفَعَهُ ٱلذِّكْرَىٰٓ ٤

[5] But, as for the one who thinks he can take care of himself,

أَمَّا مَنِ ٱسْتَغْنَىٰ ٥

[6] to him you give your attention (O Prophet)

فَأَنتَ لَهُۥ تَصَدَّىٰ ٦

[7] although you will not be blamed if he does not purify himself.

وَمَا عَلَيۡكَ أَلَّا يَزَّكَّىٰ ٧

[8] And as for the one who comes to you eagerly,

وَأَمَّا مَن جَآءَكَ يَسۡعَىٰ ٨

[9] and fears (Allah),

وَهُوَ يَخۡشَىٰ ٩

[10] from him, you are distracted.

فَأَنتَ عَنۡهُ تَلَهَّىٰ ١٠

[11] No (it should not be so.) It is a Reminder,[28]

كَلَّآ إِنَّهَا تَذۡكِرَةٞ ١١

[12] so let whoever wants to remember it (do so);

فَمَن شَآءَ ذَكَرَهُۥ ١٢

[13] it is on honoured pages,

فِي صُحُفٖ مُّكَرَّمَةٖ ١٣

[14] kept high and pure,[29]

مَّرۡفُوعَةٖ مُّطَهَّرَةِۭ ١٤

[15] (written) by the hands of scribes

بِأَيۡدِي سَفَرَةٖ ١٥

---

28. The Reminder is one of the names for the Qur'ān.

29. Allah preserves the Qur'ān in the heavens, and we should keep the written copies of the Qur'ān in a high, honoured place in our homes.

[16] who are noble and pious.[30]

كِرَامٍۭ بَرَرَةٍ ﴿١٦﴾

[17] Cursed is man; how ungrateful he is!

قُتِلَ ٱلْإِنسَٰنُ مَآ أَكْفَرَهُۥ ﴿١٧﴾

[18] From what did He create him?

مِنْ أَىِّ شَىْءٍ خَلَقَهُۥ ﴿١٨﴾

[19] From a drop of sperm[31] He created him, and moulded him in (good) proportions,

مِن نُّطْفَةٍ خَلَقَهُۥ فَقَدَّرَهُۥ ﴿١٩﴾

[20] then makes the way easy for him,

ثُمَّ ٱلسَّبِيلَ يَسَّرَهُۥ ﴿٢٠﴾

---

30. This may refer to the angels who wrote the Qur'ān according to Allah's instructions on the Preserved Tablet before it was revealed through the Angel Jibrā'īl ﵇ to Muḥammad ﷺ, or to the early Muslim scribes who carefully wrote down the revelations of Allah under the Prophet's ﷺ guidance after they were revealed, or both. Only about 45 *sūrahs* had been revealed in Makkah before this one, and this verse is one that has been used to show that the early Muslims were very careful not only to memorize but also to write down each revelation of the Qur'ān, although it was not collected into one book until after the Prophet's ﷺ death.

31. A sperm is a very tiny seed from the father which joins with an ovum, or tiny egg, from the mother, to form a human baby. At first, the new baby inside its mother cannot do anything – hear, see, or speak. After growing inside its mother for nine months, it is still very helpless at birth. We are reminded here that we all started out as very small and helpless creatures, and Allah gave us everything – the gift of life itself and everything we need to preserve it – and still there are people who do not care and are not grateful!

[21] then causes him to die and to be buried,

ثُمَّ أَمَاتَهُۥ فَأَقْبَرَهُۥ ﴿٢١﴾

[22] then, when He wills, He will raise him (to life again).

ثُمَّ إِذَا شَآءَ أَنشَرَهُۥ ﴿٢٢﴾

[23] No, surely man has not fulfilled what Allah has commanded him.

كَلَّا لَمَّا يَقْضِ مَآ أَمَرَهُۥ ﴿٢٣﴾

[24] So, let man consider his food:

فَلْيَنظُرِ ٱلْإِنسَٰنُ إِلَىٰ طَعَامِهِۦٓ ﴿٢٤﴾

[25] We pour down the water in abundant rains,

أَنَّا صَبَبْنَا ٱلْمَآءَ صَبًّا ﴿٢٥﴾

[26] then We split the earth in fissures,[32]

ثُمَّ شَقَقْنَا ٱلْأَرْضَ شَقًّا ﴿٢٦﴾

[27] and make the grains grow in them,

فَأَنۢبَتْنَا فِيهَا حَبًّا ﴿٢٧﴾

[28] and grapes and fresh green plants,

وَعِنَبًا وَقَضْبًا ﴿٢٨﴾

[29] and olives and palm trees,

وَزَيْتُونًا وَنَخْلًا ﴿٢٩﴾

---

32. Farmers must plough and loosen the soil so that the many kinds of plants can easily take root in the earth and grow. Heavy rains help in this process, loosening and cracking the soil.

[30] and gardens thick with tall trees,

وَحَدَآئِقَ غُلۡبٗا ٣٠

[31] and fruits and pastures,

وَفَٰكِهَةٗ وَأَبّٗا ٣١

[32] for the comfort of you and your flocks.

مَّتَٰعٗا لَّكُمۡ وَلِأَنۡعَٰمِكُمۡ ٣٢

[33] But when the deafening Shout comes,[33]

فَإِذَا جَآءَتِ ٱلصَّآخَّةُ ٣٣

[34] on the Day when a man shall run from his (own) brother,

يَوۡمَ يَفِرُّ ٱلۡمَرۡءُ مِنۡ أَخِيهِ ٣٤

[35] his mother, his father,

وَأُمِّهِۦ وَأَبِيهِ ٣٥

[36] and from his wife and his children,

وَصَٰحِبَتِهِۦ وَبَنِيهِ ٣٦

[37] every man, on that day, will have enough worries of his own to make him forget (everyone else).

لِكُلِّ ٱمۡرِيٕٖ مِّنۡهُمۡ يَوۡمَئِذٖ شَأۡنٞ يُغۡنِيهِ ٣٧

[38] Some faces on that Day will be shining,

وُجُوهٞ يَوۡمَئِذٖ مُّسۡفِرَةٞ ٣٨

---

33. The shout at the beginning of the Resurrection, the cry of an angel or blast of a trumpet.

[39] laughing, happy (with their good news),

ضَاحِكَةٌ مُّسْتَبْشِرَةٌ ﴿٣٩﴾

[40] and other faces on that Day will be covered with dust,

وَوُجُوهٌ يَوْمَئِذٍ عَلَيْهَا غَبَرَةٌ ﴿٤٠﴾

[41] veiled in darkness.

تَرْهَقُهَا قَتَرَةٌ ﴿٤١﴾

[42] Those are the unbelievers, the wicked.

أُوْلَٰٓئِكَ هُمُ ٱلْكَفَرَةُ ٱلْفَجَرَةُ ﴿٤٢﴾

81

at-Takwīr [The Folding Up]

MAKKAN PERIOD

This was one of the very first *sūrahs* to be revealed – perhaps the sixth or seventh. The first section uses very powerful language and images to draw people's attention to the coming Resurrection and final Judgement. These *āyahs* speak of a time when the world as we know it will be completely changed according to Allah's Divine plan and purpose.

The last section defends the revelation against the claims of the unbelievers, who either accused the Prophet Muḥammad ﷺ of being a poet, or a spiritualist in communication with the *jinn*, or a madman possessed by the devil. Of course, none of their accusations could be taken seriously; the unbelievers simply did not know what else to say about the Qur'ān because they had never heard anything like it before. Although many *sūrahs* of the Qur'ān have a certain rhyme and rhythm, they are not poetry. Muḥammad ﷺ was never known to compose poetry before he received the first revelation of the Qur'ān, and most poems written by Arabs in that time were about love or warfare. No simple poet would have dared to attack the Makkan way of life by speaking out against idolatry or other established practices such as the killing of innocent baby girls (see footnote 38 to *āyah*

9 below). On the other hand, the words and messages of people who claim to be in communication with the spirit world are usually secretive and unclear. Such people ordinarily deal with personal or trivial details of life, but the Qur'ān is a clear message to all humanity. Lastly, no one possessed by a devil or *jinn* could be expected to have the good character and noble qualities which distinguished the Prophet ﷺ from the other people of Makkah. A man inspired by a devil would not wish to convert people from worshipping idols and following the evil ways of Satan to worshipping One God and doing good. No, says the Qur'ān, this is not what you imagine; it is a clear warning and reminder from a merciful God.

at-Takwīr

[The Folding Up]

سُورَةُ التَّكْوِيرِ

In the name of Allah, the All-Merciful, the Most Kind

بِسْمِ ٱللَّهِ ٱلرَّحْمَٰنِ ٱلرَّحِيمِ

[1] When the sun is folded up,[34]

إِذَا ٱلشَّمْسُ كُوِّرَتْ ١

[2] and when the stars fall,

وَإِذَا ٱلنُّجُومُ ٱنكَدَرَتْ ٢

[3] and when the mountains vanish,

وَإِذَا ٱلْجِبَالُ سُيِّرَتْ ٣

[4] and when the pregnant camels (ready to deliver their young) are abandoned,[35]

وَإِذَا ٱلْعِشَارُ عُطِّلَتْ ٤

[5] and when the wild animals are herded together,

وَإِذَا ٱلْوُحُوشُ حُشِرَتْ ٥

---

34. *Kuwwirat* means folded or twisted, like a sheet or turban; here it can also mean when the sun is darkened.

35. Camels have traditionally been highly valued by the Bedouin Arabs because they have needed them in order to survive in the harsh desert. Camels provide meat, milk, hair for tents and weaving, a means of easy transportation through the sand, and more. Pregnant camels who are about to deliver their young are very carefully watched by their keepers, but on the Day of Judgement people will be too distracted by the terrible events to pay any attention to them.

[6] and when the oceans are on fire,[36]

وَإِذَا ٱلْبِحَارُ سُجِّرَتْ ﴿٦﴾

[7] and when the souls are reunited,[37]

وَإِذَا ٱلنُّفُوسُ زُوِّجَتْ ﴿٧﴾

[8] and when the baby girl who was buried alive is asked

وَإِذَا ٱلْمَوْءُۥدَةُ سُئِلَتْ ﴿٨﴾

[9] for what crime she was killed,[38]

بِأَىِّ ذَنۢبٍ قُتِلَتْ ﴿٩﴾

[10] and when the scrolls[39] are spread open,

وَإِذَا ٱلصُّحُفُ نُشِرَتْ ﴿١٠﴾

---

36. Or when the oceans boil over, or overflow and mingle with each other.

37. This can mean when the souls are reunited with their bodies, or when the souls are sorted into groups, good and bad.

38. The Arabs in the days before Islam often used to kill their baby girls by burying them alive when they thought that they would not have enough food to feed them. They believed that sons were better than daughters because of their status and economic value in society (sons would grow up to help their fathers, but girls would leave their families to marry and help their husbands; therefore they were considered a 'wasted investment'). They treated their daughters badly even if they let them live. Allah, of course, declared this to be *ḥarām*. Believers should never kill their children out of fear of poverty or any other reason – either before birth, as in abortion, or after birth.

39. Scroll – a roll of parchment or paper. People used to record important things on one long piece of paper, rolled up on a stick, until they learned to make books. Most scholars say that the scrolls mentioned in this verse are the books of each person's deeds, which will be open for everyone to see.

[11] and when the sky is torn off,

وَإِذَا ٱلسَّمَآءُ كُشِطَتۡ ١١

[12] and when Hell is set to blaze,

وَإِذَا ٱلۡجَحِيمُ سُعِّرَتۡ ١٢

[13] and when the Garden is brought near,

وَإِذَا ٱلۡجَنَّةُ أُزۡلِفَتۡ ١٣

[14] (then) every soul will know what it has prepared (for itself).

عَلِمَتۡ نَفۡسٞ مَّآ أَحۡضَرَتۡ ١٤

[15] So, I call to witness the planets that recede,[40]

فَلَآ أُقۡسِمُ بِٱلۡخُنَّسِ ١٥

[16] and rise and set,

ٱلۡجَوَارِ ٱلۡكُنَّسِ ١٦

[17] and the night as it darkens,

وَٱلَّيۡلِ إِذَا عَسۡعَسَ ١٧

[18] and the dawn as it breathes (away the darkness),

وَٱلصُّبۡحِ إِذَا تَنَفَّسَ ١٨

---

40. Recede – to move backwards, as the planets seem to do in the night sky from the point of view of someone observing from earth.

[19] that this is truly the word of a noble Messenger (from Allah),[41]	إِنَّهُۥ لَقَوۡلُ رَسُولٖ كَرِيمٖ ١٩
[20] he (Jibrā'īl) is powerful, and has a place of honour with the Lord of the Throne,	ذِي قُوَّةٍ عِندَ ذِي ٱلۡعَرۡشِ مَكِينٖ ٢٠
[21] he is obeyed[42] and trustworthy.	مُّطَاعٖ ثَمَّ أَمِينٖ ٢١
[22] And your companion (Muḥammad) is not crazy.[43]	وَمَا صَاحِبُكُم بِمَجۡنُونٖ ٢٢
[23] He saw him (Jibrā'īl)[44] without any doubt, on the clear horizon,	وَلَقَدۡ رَءَاهُ بِٱلۡأُفُقِ ٱلۡمُبِينِ ٢٣
[24] and he is not hiding anything of the Unseen,	وَمَا هُوَ عَلَى ٱلۡغَيۡبِ بِضَنِينٖ ٢٤

41. The noble messenger here is the Angel Jibrā'īl عليه السلام. This does not mean that the Qur'ān is Jibrā'īl's own words; he is an angel-messenger bringing Allah's words to humans.

42. The Angel Jibrā'īl عليه السلام is obeyed by the other angels in the heavens.

43. Crazy, mad, or possessed by a devil.

[25] and this is not the speech of a cursed devil.	وَمَا هُوَ بِقَوْلِ شَيْطَٰنٍ رَّجِيمٍ ٢٥
[26] Where, then, are you going?	فَأَيْنَ تَذْهَبُونَ ٢٦
[27] This is no less than a Reminder to all creation,	إِنْ هُوَ إِلَّا ذِكْرٌ لِّلْعَٰلَمِينَ ٢٧
[28] to those of you who wish to walk straight;	لِمَن شَآءَ مِنكُمْ أَن يَسْتَقِيمَ ٢٨
[29] and you will not wish to unless Allah wills – the Lord of the Worlds.	وَمَا تَشَآءُونَ إِلَّآ أَن يَشَآءَ ٱللَّهُ رَبُّ ٱلْعَٰلَمِينَ ٢٩

---

44. The Prophet Muḥammad ﷺ saw the Angel Jibrā'īl عليه السلام in his original form as Allah created him, on the day of the first Revelation outside of the cave at Ḥirā'.

82

al-Infiṭār [The Shattering]

MAKKAN PERIOD

This is another *sūrah* in a series which discusses the Day of Resurrection and the Judgement. The Prophet ﷺ said: 'He who wishes to see the Day of Resurrection as though he is seeing it with his own eyes, should read *sūrahs at-Takwīr, al-Infiṭār* and *al-Inshiqāq.*'[45] These three *sūrahs* give an accurate and realistic view of what that fearful time will be like.

Often, people feel that they are powerful during their lives on earth. In their roles as businessmen or community leaders, or because they think that they are stronger, smarter, older, richer, famous or more beautiful than others, they often have a false sense of security. Perhaps they feel that whatever bad deeds they have done, secretly or openly, will not be noticed or remembered. Perhaps they become used to having their own way because of their ability to bully others with brute force, convince them with clever arguments or bribe them with their wealth.

On Judgement Day, all of this will change and true justice will prevail. People will be surprised to discover that everything they have thought and done, both large and small, has been recorded by angels. More than that, they

45. *Ḥadīth* from the collection of Tirmidhī.

will not be able to influence that Judgement one bit.

Fathers will not be able to help their sons with their wealth, nor will friends be able to help each other with their 'connections'. Each person will stand alone, unable to deny what he or she has done, and the absolute power on that Day will be in Allah's hands.

al-Infiṭār

[The Shattering]

سُورَةُ الانفِطَار

In the name of Allah, the All-Merciful, the Most Kind

بِسْمِ ٱللَّهِ ٱلرَّحْمَٰنِ ٱلرَّحِيمِ

[1] When the sky is shattered,

إِذَا ٱلسَّمَآءُ ٱنفَطَرَتْ ١

[2] when the stars are scattered,

وَإِذَا ٱلْكَوَاكِبُ ٱنتَثَرَتْ ٢

[3] when the oceans burst,[46]

وَإِذَا ٱلْبِحَارُ فُجِّرَتْ ٣

[4] and the graves are overturned,[47]

وَإِذَا ٱلْقُبُورُ بُعْثِرَتْ ٤

[5] (then) each soul will know what it has sent ahead and what it has left behind.[48]

عَلِمَتْ نَفْسٌ مَّا قَدَّمَتْ
وَأَخَّرَتْ ٥

---

46. This either means that the earth's sweet water and salty seas will be mixed together, or that the oceans will rise and cover the land.

47. The graves will be turned upside down and opened or emptied when the dead are resurrected to life.

48. Our deeds, good and bad, are what we send ahead for our next life; our family and possessions are what we leave behind.

[6] O human! What has deceived you about your Lord, the Generous One

يَٰٓأَيُّهَا ٱلْإِنسَٰنُ مَا غَرَّكَ بِرَبِّكَ ٱلْكَرِيمِ ٦

[7] Who created you, and shaped you in perfect balance and proportion,[49]

ٱلَّذِى خَلَقَكَ فَسَوَّىٰكَ فَعَدَلَكَ ٧

[8] and fashioned you in whatever form He pleased?

فِىٓ أَىِّ صُورَةٍ مَّا شَآءَ رَكَّبَكَ ٨

[9] No, but you deny the Judgement,

كَلَّا بَلْ تُكَذِّبُونَ بِٱلدِّينِ ٩

[10] yet surely there are guardian (angels) over you,

وَإِنَّ عَلَيْكُمْ لَحَٰفِظِينَ ١٠

[11] noble (angels) who write down (your actions),

كِرَامًا كَٰتِبِينَ ١١

---

49. Allah has created humans as balanced and well-proportioned creatures: unlike some animals with very long noses but tiny eyes, or those who can hear very well or run very fast but are lacking other abilities, people have been gifted with all of the senses and body parts in beautiful proportion to each other. We have the possibility to develop our physical, mental, emotional and spiritual faculties to great heights; we can adapt ourselves to a great variety of environments from the tropics to icy polar regions, and so forth. The superior potential of humans over other creatures has very much to do with this perfect balance and proportion.

[12] who know all that you do.

يَعۡلَمُونَ مَا تَفۡعَلُونَ ١٢

[13] As for the righteous, they will be in great happiness,

إِنَّ ٱلۡأَبۡرَارَ لَفِي نَعِيمٖ ١٣

[14] and the wicked will be in Hell.

وَإِنَّ ٱلۡفُجَّارَ لَفِي جَحِيمٖ ١٤

[15] They will enter it on the Day of Judgement,

يَصۡلَوۡنَهَا يَوۡمَ ٱلدِّينِ ١٥

[16] and they shall never escape from it.

وَمَا هُمۡ عَنۡهَا بِغَآئِبِينَ ١٦

[17] Oh, what can make you understand what the Day of Judgement is?

وَمَآ أَدۡرَىٰكَ مَا يَوۡمُ ٱلدِّينِ ١٧

[18] Again, what can make you understand what the Day of Judgement is?

ثُمَّ مَآ أَدۡرَىٰكَ مَا يَوۡمُ ٱلدِّينِ ١٨

[19] A day when no soul is able to help another soul in any way, and the absolute command on that day belongs to Allah.

يَوۡمَ لَا تَمۡلِكُ نَفۡسٞ لِّنَفۡسٖ شَيۡـٔٗاۖ
وَٱلۡأَمۡرُ يَوۡمَئِذٖ لِّلَّهِ ١٩

83

al-Muṭaffifīn [The Cheaters]

MAKKAN PERIOD

This *sūrah* is named after people who try to win over others through cheating, trickery, the abuse of power, and other unjust methods. The first section of the *sūrah* condemns people who try to gain something for themselves at the expense of others, by using a 'double-standard'. This practice is especially common among shopkeepers, traders and businessmen who try to do everything within their power – evading taxes, using cheap materials, hiding defects in their products, false advertising, and so forth – in order to make more money. We must remember to be as fair in our dealings with all people as we would like them to be with us, and also to be kind, as we hope that Allah will be kind to us on the Last Day. As Muslims who are trying to achieve good behaviour, we should be fair and just to others even when they are not fair to us, and should avoid using our positions to gain advantages for ourselves, our friends or our families. Rather, we should view every human being as a relative, a member of the family of the Children of Adam ﷺ. The Prophet ﷺ has said: 'No one is a (true) believer until he wishes for his brother what he wishes for himself.'[50]

50. *Ḥadīth* from the collection of Muslim.

The second part of the *sūrah* continues the theme of Judgement Day. The book of *Sijjīn* is a kind of collective prison record of all the worst crimes committed by people (not their individual book of deeds). Out of disrespect, it will be placed in the lowest part of Hellfire. Its opposite, the book of *'Illīyīn,* is a record of all the best actions of the believers, and is kept in a high place in Paradise where the angels and people who are close to Allah can read it. The people of Paradise will be given a very special drink – a nectar better than the best wine that unbelievers boast of on earth – which has been mixed with pure water from the fountain of *Tasnīm*, which is in an elevated place in Paradise. This special drink will be sealed with a wonderful musk perfume, and will give refreshment and pleasure without the drunkenness or harmful effects of earthly wine.

al-Muṭaffifīn

[The Cheaters]

سُورَةُ المُطَفِّفِينَ

In the name of Allah, the All-Merciful, the Most Kind

بِسْمِ ٱللَّهِ ٱلرَّحْمَٰنِ ٱلرَّحِيمِ

[1] Oh, ruined are the cheaters!

وَيْلٌ لِّلْمُطَفِّفِينَ ١

[2] – those who, when they measure out what others owe them, demand it all,

ٱلَّذِينَ إِذَا ٱكْتَالُوا۟ عَلَى ٱلنَّاسِ يَسْتَوْفُونَ ٢

[3] but when they measure out (what they owe) to others, they hold some back.

وَإِذَا كَالُوهُمْ أَو وَّزَنُوهُمْ يُخْسِرُونَ ٣

[4] Do these people not realise that they will be raised (from the dead)

أَلَا يَظُنُّ أُو۟لَٰٓئِكَ أَنَّهُم مَّبْعُوثُونَ ٤

[5] for a Mighty Day,

لِيَوْمٍ عَظِيمٍ ٥

[6] the Day on which all mankind will stand before the Lord of all the Worlds?

يَوْمَ يَقُومُ ٱلنَّاسُ لِرَبِّ ٱلْعَٰلَمِينَ ٦

[7] No (they are mistaken), but truly, the record of the evil ones is in *Sijjīn*.[51]

كَلَّآ إِنَّ كِتَٰبَ ٱلْفُجَّارِ لَفِى
سِجِّينٍ ٧

[8] And what can make you understand what *Sijjīn* is?

وَمَآ أَدْرَىٰكَ مَا سِجِّينٌ ٨

[9] A book written (in detail about them).[52]

كِتَٰبٌ مَّرْقُومٌ ٩

[10] The liars will be in trouble on that day!

وَيْلٌ يَوْمَئِذٍ لِّلْمُكَذِّبِينَ ١٠

[11] Those that deny the Day of Judgement,

ٱلَّذِينَ يُكَذِّبُونَ بِيَوْمِ ٱلدِّينِ ١١

[12] which no one would deny except the very sinful ones who pass the limits,

وَمَا يُكَذِّبُ بِهِۦٓ إِلَّا كُلُّ مُعْتَدٍ
أَثِيمٍ ١٢

[13] who, when Our verses are recited to him, says: 'These are just stories from the old days!'

إِذَا تُتْلَىٰ عَلَيْهِ ءَايَٰتُنَا قَالَ أَسَٰطِيرُ
ٱلْأَوَّلِينَ ١٣

[14] No (they are mistaken), but the things they have done have put rust on their hearts.

كَلَّا ۖ بَلْ ۜ رَانَ عَلَىٰ قُلُوبِهِم مَّا كَانُوا۟
يَكْسِبُونَ ١٤

---

51. *Sijjīn* comes from the word *sajana* which means to put in prison.
52. See the explanation of *Sijjīn* in the introduction to the *sūrah*.

[15] No, and surely on that day they will be veiled from their Lord;

كَلَّآ إِنَّهُمۡ عَن رَّبِّهِمۡ يَوۡمَئِذٖ لَّمَحۡجُوبُونَ ١٥

[16] then they surely will burn in Hell,

ثُمَّ إِنَّهُمۡ لَصَالُواْ ٱلۡجَحِيمِ ١٦

[17] and it will be said to them, 'This is what you used to deny.'

ثُمَّ يُقَالُ هَٰذَا ٱلَّذِي كُنتُم بِهِۦ تُكَذِّبُونَ ١٧

[18] No, but surely the record of the good ones is in *'Illīyīn.*

كَلَّآ إِنَّ كِتَٰبَ ٱلۡأَبۡرَارِ لَفِي عِلِّيِّينَ ١٨

[19] And what can make you understand what *'Illīyīn*[53] is?

وَمَآ أَدۡرَىٰكَ مَا عِلِّيُّونَ ١٩

[20] A book written (in detail about them),

كِتَٰبٞ مَّرۡقُومٞ ٢٠

[21] witnessed by those who are near (to Allah).

يَشۡهَدُهُ ٱلۡمُقَرَّبُونَ ٢١

[22] Truly, the good ones will be in great happiness,

إِنَّ ٱلۡأَبۡرَارَ لَفِي نَعِيمٍ ٢٢

---

53. Literally, *'Illīyūn*, a grammatical variation of *'Illīyīn*, which means 'high places' in Arabic.

[23] on couches, gazing (in wonder);[54]

عَلَى ٱلْأَرَآئِكِ يَنظُرُونَ ﴿٢٣﴾

[24] you will see in their faces the beaming radiance of true delight

تَعْرِفُ فِى وُجُوهِهِمْ نَضْرَةَ ٱلنَّعِيمِ ﴿٢٤﴾

[25] as they are given a drink of pure nectar, sealed,

يُسْقَوْنَ مِن رَّحِيقٍ مَّخْتُومٍ ﴿٢٥﴾

[26] whose seal is musk; let those who strive for great achievements strive for this!

خِتَٰمُهُۥ مِسْكٌ ۚ وَفِى ذَٰلِكَ
فَلْيَتَنَافَسِ ٱلْمُتَنَٰفِسُونَ ﴿٢٦﴾

[27] (The pure nectar is) mixed with water of *Tasnīm*,

وَمِزَاجُهُۥ مِن تَسْنِيمٍ ﴿٢٧﴾

[28] a fountain where those who are nearest (to Allah) drink.

عَيْنًا يَشْرَبُ بِهَا ٱلْمُقَرَّبُونَ ﴿٢٨﴾

[29] The sinners used to laugh at the believers,

إِنَّ ٱلَّذِينَ أَجْرَمُوا۟ كَانُوا۟ مِنَ ٱلَّذِينَ
ءَامَنُوا۟ يَضْحَكُونَ ﴿٢٩﴾

---

54. The people of Paradise will be gazing in wonder at all that they have been given. They may also be gazing at Allah's Divine Face, since the unbelievers will be denied this privilege according to verse 15.

[30] and wink to each other (making fun) when they passed them,

وَإِذَا مَرُّوا۟ بِهِمْ يَتَغَامَزُونَ ٣٠

[31] and when they returned to their own people, they came telling jokes about them,

وَإِذَا ٱنقَلَبُوٓا۟ إِلَىٰٓ أَهْلِهِمُ ٱنقَلَبُوا۟
فَكِهِينَ ٣١

[32] and when they saw them, they said, 'Those people are really confused.'

وَإِذَا رَأَوْهُمْ قَالُوٓا۟ إِنَّ هَٰٓؤُلَآءِ
لَضَآلُّونَ ٣٢

[33] Even though they were not sent to be in charge, watching over them.

وَمَآ أُرْسِلُوا۟ عَلَيْهِمْ حَٰفِظِينَ ٣٣

[34] But on this Day, the believers will laugh at the deniers (of the Judgement);[55]

فَٱلْيَوْمَ ٱلَّذِينَ ءَامَنُوا۟ مِنَ ٱلْكُفَّارِ
يَضْحَكُونَ ٣٤

[35] on couches, gazing (in wonder).

عَلَى ٱلْأَرَآئِكِ يَنظُرُونَ ٣٥

[36] Will the unbelievers not be paid back for what they used to do?

هَلْ ثُوِّبَ ٱلْكُفَّارُ مَا كَانُوا۟
يَفْعَلُونَ ٣٦

---

55. The believers used to be teased and joked about on earth, but in Paradise it is they who will have the 'last laugh'.

84

al-Inshiqāq [The Splitting Apart]

MAKKAN PERIOD

This is another *sūrah* treating the topic of the Resurrection, similar to *Sūrah* 82, *al-Infiṭār.* It begins with some of the signs of Judgement Day, when all that was covered up will be shown and all that was hidden will be known. The earth will reveal all that is within her, according to Allah's order.

Sūrat al-Inshiqāq goes on to describe the handing out of the books of deeds on Judgement Day. Each human being has two angels, one on the left side and one on the right side, who write down everything he thinks, says, and does throughout his entire life. The angel on the right records the good deeds, and the angel on the left records the bad deeds. This 'super video-recording' or detailed book is given to him on Judgement Day as a reminder of what he has done.

Two main groups of people are described in this *sūrah*:

1. Those who believed in One God and His Messengers, and tried to live good lives according to God's Law; they will receive their book of deeds in their right hands and be rewarded with eternal life in Paradise. Although they may have committed many minor sins and mistakes, Allah will overlook their bad deeds and forgive them,

letting them off with an easy reckoning.

2. Those who disbelieved in God and His Messengers, and lived sinful lives; they will receive their book of deeds in their left hands or behind their backs.[56] They will wish that they could die or somehow escape their punishment, but they will be sent to the Hellfire. Some scholars have said that the reason why some unbelievers will receive their books behind their backs is that they will realize their fate before their books are given to them; out of embarrassment and shame, they will put their hands behind their backs so that they do not have to receive their books in their left hands in front of everyone.

Although these will be the two main groups of people on Judgement Day, a third (smaller) group is mentioned in *Sūrat al-Wāqiʿah* 56:10-26: those in the front, or the 'winners of the race'. These are the Prophets, saints, martyrs, great teachers and those people who have become so close to Allah through their constant worship, good deeds and struggle in the cause of Islam that they are speeded into Paradise in the twinkling of an eye or as though on wings, without needing to wait for questioning.[57]

---

56. According to *Sūrat al-Ḥāqqah* 69: 25.
57. Based on a *ḥadīth* from the collection of Muslim.

al-Inshiqāq

[The Splitting Apart]

سُورَةُ الانشِقَاقِ

In the name of Allah, the All-Merciful, the Most Kind

بِسۡمِ ٱللَّهِ ٱلرَّحۡمَٰنِ ٱلرَّحِيمِ

[1] When the sky is split apart,[58]

إِذَا ٱلسَّمَآءُ ٱنشَقَّتۡ ١

[2] and listens to (the command of) her Lord, as she must,

وَأَذِنَتۡ لِرَبِّهَا وَحُقَّتۡ ٢

[3] and when the earth is stretched,

وَإِذَا ٱلۡأَرۡضُ مُدَّتۡ ٣

[4] and throws out all that is inside her, becoming empty,

وَأَلۡقَتۡ مَا فِيهَا وَتَخَلَّتۡ ٤

[5] and listens to (the command of) her Lord, as she must: (then you will realize).

وَأَذِنَتۡ لِرَبِّهَا وَحُقَّتۡ ٥

---

58. On the Day of Resurrection.

[6] O human! Surely you are working toward your Lord with hard labour, but you will meet Him.

يَـٰٓأَيُّهَا ٱلْإِنسَـٰنُ إِنَّكَ كَادِحٌ إِلَىٰ
رَبِّكَ كَدْحًا فَمُلَـٰقِيهِ ٦

[7] Then, as for the one who is given his book (of deeds) in his right hand,

فَأَمَّا مَنْ أُوتِىَ كِتَـٰبَهُۥ بِيَمِينِهِۦ ٧

[8] he will be given an easy reckoning

فَسَوْفَ يُحَاسَبُ حِسَابًا يَسِيرًا ٨

[9] and he will return to his people in joy.

وَيَنقَلِبُ إِلَىٰٓ أَهْلِهِۦ مَسْرُورًا ٩

[10] As for the one who is given his book (of deeds) behind his back,

وَأَمَّا مَنْ أُوتِىَ كِتَـٰبَهُۥ وَرَآءَ
ظَهْرِهِۦ ١٠

[11] he will ask to be destroyed (rather than suffer punishment);

فَسَوْفَ يَدْعُوا۟ ثُبُورًا ١١

[12] but he will burn in a blazing Fire.

وَيَصْلَىٰ سَعِيرًا ١٢

[13] Really, he used to go around happily among his people;

إِنَّهُۥ كَانَ فِىٓ أَهْلِهِۦ مَسْرُورًا ١٣

[14] he thought he would never return (to Allah).

إِنَّهُۥ ظَنَّ أَن لَّن يَحُورَ ١٤

[15] No, never! For his Lord was always watching over him.

بَلَىٰٓ إِنَّ رَبَّهُۥ كَانَ بِهِۦ بَصِيرًا ١٥

[16] No, but I swear by the glow of the sunset,

فَلَآ أُقۡسِمُ بِٱلشَّفَقِ ١٦

[17] and the night and all that it enfolds,[59]

وَٱلَّيۡلِ وَمَا وَسَقَ ١٧

[18] and the moon when it is full,

وَٱلۡقَمَرِ إِذَا ٱتَّسَقَ ١٨

[19] that you shall travel on from stage to stage.[60]

لَتَرۡكَبُنَّ طَبَقًا عَن طَبَقٖ ١٩

---

59. 'Gathers together', 'enfolds' or 'enshrouds'. Night is the time when people return to their homes, animals are gathered in barns; creatures are brought together with each other.

60. According to scholars, this may refer to several things: firstly, the stages of the human life cycle, from life inside the mother, to birth, childhood, adulthood, old age, death, and life after death. Secondly, to the spiritual growth of a believer as he or she increases in faith and practice, which is often described as a journey in stages. It may also mean that Muslims will have to be patient with increasingly difficult conditions in this life and the Next.

[20] What is the matter with them, that they do not believe?

فَمَا لَهُمْ لَا يُؤْمِنُونَ ﴿٢٠﴾

[21] and when the Qur'ān is recited to them, they do not fall prostrate?[61]

وَإِذَا قُرِئَ عَلَيْهِمُ ٱلْقُرْءَانُ
لَا يَسْجُدُونَ ۩ ﴿٢١﴾

[22] No, but the unbelievers reject (it)

بَلِ ٱلَّذِينَ كَفَرُوا۟ يُكَذِّبُونَ ﴿٢٢﴾

[23] and Allah knows best what they hide.

وَٱللَّهُ أَعْلَمُ بِمَا يُوعُونَ ﴿٢٣﴾

[24] So give them good news[62] of a painful punishment,

فَبَشِّرْهُم بِعَذَابٍ أَلِيمٍ ﴿٢٤﴾

[25] except those who believe and do good, for they shall have a reward unending.

إِلَّا ٱلَّذِينَ ءَامَنُوا۟ وَعَمِلُوا۟
ٱلصَّـٰلِحَـٰتِ لَهُمْ أَجْرٌ غَيْرُ
مَمْنُونٍۭ ﴿٢٥﴾

---

61. Prostrate – to make *sajdah*, touching our faces, hands and knees to the ground, as we do in prayer. This is one of the 14 places in the Qur'ān where we must stop and prostrate ourselves if we recite it or hear it being recited in Arabic.

62. 'Good news' is used here in a mocking way.

85

al-Burūj [The Constellations]

MAKKAN PERIOD

This *sūrah* is named after the twelve constellations, or groups of stars, which appear to rotate in the night sky throughout the year. The opening verses refer to the Judgement, and the promised Day means the Day of Judgement. According to Ibn 'Abbās ☙ the 'witness and what is witnessed' means Allah and all of His creation; in other words, Allah sees everything that every creature does. According to 'Alī ☙, 'the witness' means the Prophet Muḥammad ﷺ and his *ummah* are those who 'are witnessed'. This opinion is based on another verse in the Qur'ān which says: 'How will it be when We produce a witness from every nation, and We call on you (Muḥammad) to testify against them?' (*an-Nisā'* 4: 41).

The *sūrah* then goes on to speak of an ancient people who persecuted believers by burning them alive. Different stories are told about who these people might be, but most scholars believe that it refers to a Jewish King of the city of Najrān in Yemen named Dhū Nuwās. He was said to have thrown many hundreds or thousands of sincere Christians in his city into a large trench or pit filled with fire, burning them alive in an effort to try to get them to give up their new religion.[63]

Sūrat al-Burūj was revealed at a time when the Muslims were being heavily persecuted by the unbelievers of Makkah. The story of the 'People of the Pit of fire' thus carried with it a message and a lesson. It encouraged the believers who were suffering persecution to remain patient and strong, and feel confident of Allah's reward. At the same time, it warned those who harm others simply because of their faith that their own punishment would be coming in due time. Those unbelievers who tortured believers with fire will themselves end up in the blazing fire of Hell. The *sūrah* ends by reminding the unbelievers of Makkah, who felt themselves to be very powerful, that even the Pharaoh of Egypt with his huge army could not avoid his fate. Allah surrounds everyone, and He is Mightiest – but He is also the Most Forgiving to those who seek His forgiveness.

---

63. For historical evidence to confirm this story, which is said to have happened in the year 523 of the Christian Era (AD), see Mawdūdī's *The Meaning of the Qur'ān*, Vol. XV, Islamic Publications, Lahore, 1987. Other scholars believe that these verses may refer to the Biblical story of Nebuchadnezzar, who tried without success to burn three pious Jews in a fiery furnace (see Daniel 3: 19-30).

al-Burūj

[The Constellations]

سُورَةُ البُرُوجِ

In the name of Allah, the All-Merciful, the Most Kind

بِسْمِ ٱللَّهِ ٱلرَّحْمَٰنِ ٱلرَّحِيمِ

[1] By the (night) sky with its constellations,

وَٱلسَّمَآءِ ذَاتِ ٱلْبُرُوجِ ١

[2] and by the promised Day,

وَٱلْيَوْمِ ٱلْمَوْعُودِ ٢

[3] and by the witness and what is witnessed:

وَشَاهِدٍ وَمَشْهُودٍ ٣

[4] ruined are the People of the Pit (of fire) –

قُتِلَ أَصْحَٰبُ ٱلْأُخْدُودِ ٤

[5] it was blazing with fuel

ٱلنَّارِ ذَاتِ ٱلْوَقُودِ ٥

[6] when they sat by it,

إِذْ هُمْ عَلَيْهَا قُعُودٌ ٦

[7] and they witnessed for themselves what they were doing to the believers;

وَهُمْ عَلَىٰ مَا يَفْعَلُونَ بِٱلْمُؤْمِنِينَ
شُهُودٌ ٧

[8] and they had nothing against them except that they believed in Allah, the Mighty, the Praised,

وَمَا نَقَمُوا۟ مِنْهُمْ إِلَّآ أَن يُؤْمِنُوا۟
بِٱللَّهِ ٱلْعَزِيزِ ٱلْحَمِيدِ ٨

[9] Whose kingdom is the heavens and the earth. And Allah is a Witness to all things.

ٱلَّذِى لَهُۥ مُلْكُ ٱلسَّمَٰوَٰتِ وَٱلْأَرْضِ ۚ
وَٱللَّهُ عَلَىٰ كُلِّ شَىْءٍ شَهِيدٌ ٩

[10] Surely those who persecute believing men and women and do not repent shall have the punishment of Hell. They shall have the punishment of burning.

إِنَّ ٱلَّذِينَ فَتَنُوا۟ ٱلْمُؤْمِنِينَ وَٱلْمُؤْمِنَٰتِ
ثُمَّ لَمْ يَتُوبُوا۟ فَلَهُمْ عَذَابُ جَهَنَّمَ
وَلَهُمْ عَذَابُ ٱلْحَرِيقِ ١٠

[11] But for those who believe and do good deeds, there will be Gardens in which rivers flow.That is the great victory.

إِنَّ ٱلَّذِينَ ءَامَنُوا۟ وَعَمِلُوا۟ ٱلصَّٰلِحَٰتِ
لَهُمْ جَنَّٰتٌ تَجْرِى مِن تَحْتِهَا
ٱلْأَنْهَٰرُ ۚ ذَٰلِكَ ٱلْفَوْزُ ٱلْكَبِيرُ ١١

[12] Truly the grip of your Lord is mighty, powerful.

إِنَّ بَطْشَ رَبِّكَ لَشَدِيدٌ ١٢

[13] It is He Who creates and then brings back (to life),

إِنَّهُۥ هُوَ يُبْدِئُ وَيُعِيدُ ١٣

[14] and He is the Forgiving, the Loving,

وَهُوَ ٱلْغَفُورُ ٱلْوَدُودُ ١٤

[15] Lord of the Glorious Throne,

ذُو ٱلْعَرْشِ ٱلْمَجِيدُ ١٥

[16] Who does all that He wills.

فَعَّالٌ لِّمَا يُرِيدُ ١٦

[17] Have you heard the story of the armed forces

هَلْ أَتَىٰكَ حَدِيثُ ٱلْجُنُودِ ١٧

[18] of Pharaoh and Thamūd?[64]

فِرْعَوْنَ وَثَمُودَ ١٨

[19] No, but the unbelievers (still) deny (the truth)

بَلِ ٱلَّذِينَ كَفَرُوا۟ فِى تَكْذِيبٍ ١٩

[20] although Allah surrounds them (everywhere) from behind.

وَٱللَّهُ مِن وَرَآئِهِم مُّحِيطٌۢ ٢٠

[21] No, but it is a glorious Qur'ān

بَلْ هُوَ قُرْءَانٌ مَّجِيدٌ ٢١

[22] in a Guarded Tablet.

فِى لَوْحٍ مَّحْفُوظٍۭ ٢٢

---

64. The story of the Prophet Mūsā عليه السلام and Pharaoh's armies, and of the people of Thamūd occurs many times in the Qur'ān.

86

aṭ-Ṭāriq [The Night Visitor]

MAKKAN PERIOD

This *sūrah* is named after a word from the first two verses, which means something which comes at night, or knocks. Most scholars believe that it refers to a star, such as the morning star. It can also symbolise the light of faith which pierces through the darkness of unbelief or despair.

Several themes are brought out in this *sūrah*. It was revealed to the Prophet ﷺ at a time of great difficulties, and came as an assurance. In the midst of darkness, a bright star is a symbol of light and hope. Although the unbelievers were plotting against the Prophet ﷺ and his small community of believers, Allah reminded the Muslims that He knows all secret thoughts and plots, and He is the best of planners. He has assigned guardian angels to each soul to watch and record their every deed, and one day all secrets will be revealed.

Here, as in other *sūrahs* about the Resurrection, it explains that the One Who can create a baby from a tiny sperm cell and an egg can certainly bring the dead to life again. It urges the unbelievers to think again before continuing their oppression; one day they will stand before Allah for trial and no one will be able to protect them. Allah has not sent the Qur'ān as a joke or for entertainment, but in order to make things clear to people so that they may choose the best way for themselves.

The symbol of new life sprouting from humble beginnings against difficult odds is hinted at in several verses. Just as a small ray of light pierces and overcomes the darkness, the tiny sperm cell splits through the covering of a mother's egg to make a baby, and a small seed swells with water and cracks the very earth as it sprouts, so did the small, poor and weak community of Muslims overcome incredible obstacles to spread Allah's message of peace and hope across the Arabian peninsula, and eventually throughout the world.

aṭ-Ṭāriq

[The Night Visitor]

سُورَةُ الطَّارِقِ

In the name of Allah, the All-Merciful, the Most Kind

بِسۡمِ ٱللَّهِ ٱلرَّحۡمَٰنِ ٱلرَّحِيمِ

[1] By the sky and the night visitor . . .

وَٱلسَّمَآءِ وَٱلطَّارِقِ ١

[2] Ah, what will tell you what the night visitor is?

وَمَآ أَدۡرَىٰكَ مَا ٱلطَّارِقُ ٢

[3] The star of piercing brightness!

ٱلنَّجۡمُ ٱلثَّاقِبُ ٣

[4] There is no soul without a guardian watching over it.

إِن كُلُّ نَفۡسٖ لَّمَّا عَلَيۡهَا حَافِظٞ ٤

[5] So let the human think about what he is created out of.

فَلۡيَنظُرِ ٱلۡإِنسَٰنُ مِمَّ خُلِقَ ٥

[6] He is created from a gushing fluid

خُلِقَ مِن مَّآءٖ دَافِقٖ ٦

[7] which emerges from between the backbone and the breast.[65]

يَخْرُجُ مِنۢ بَيْنِ ٱلصُّلْبِ وَٱلتَّرَآئِبِ ٧

[8] Surely He is Able to bring him back (to life);

إِنَّهُۥ عَلَىٰ رَجْعِهِۦ لَقَادِرٌ ٨

[9] on the Day when the secrets will be made known,

يَوْمَ تُبْلَى ٱلسَّرَآئِرُ ٩

[10] he will have no strength or helper.

فَمَا لَهُۥ مِن قُوَّةٍ وَلَا نَاصِرٍ ١٠

[11] By the heavens which return (the rain),[66]

وَٱلسَّمَآءِ ذَاتِ ٱلرَّجْعِ ١١

[12] and the earth which splits (as the plants sprout through),

وَٱلْأَرْضِ ذَاتِ ٱلصَّدْعِ ١٢

---

65. 'The backbone' and 'the breast' symbolise the parts of man and woman that come together to make a baby.

66. This refers to the earth's water cycle. The water comes from the clouds, falls to earth and soaks and splits the soil, preparing it for plant growth. Some becomes part of the ground-water or rivers and streams, before eventually evaporating into the air, making new clouds. Allah can bring people back to life from the dead, just like He causes the rain which has fallen into the ground to rise again, rejoining the clouds.

[13] surely this (Qur'ān) is a decisive Word;[67]

إِنَّهُۥ لَقَوۡلٞ فَصۡلٞ ١٣

[14] it is not a joke.

وَمَا هُوَ بِٱلۡهَزۡلِ ١٤

[15] They are plotting (against you, Muḥammad),

إِنَّهُمۡ يَكِيدُونَ كَيۡدٗا ١٥

[16] and I (too) am plotting.

وَأَكِيدُ كَيۡدٗا ١٦

[17] So give the unbelievers a break; be easy on them for a while.

فَمَهِّلِ ٱلۡكَٰفِرِينَ أَمۡهِلۡهُمۡ
رُوَيۡدَۢا ١٧

---

67. 'The Qur'ān is a 'decisive Word': it makes things clear; distinguishes between right and wrong.

87

al-A'lā [The Most High]

MAKKAN PERIOD

This beautiful *sūrah* is one of the earliest to be revealed, and it is related on the authority of 'Alī ﵁ that the Prophet ﷺ especially loved it. He used to recite it during *ṣalāt al-witr* regularly.[68]

The beginning describes Allah's qualities as *Rabb,* the Lord of Creation. He has made everything in perfect harmony, measures out the *rizq* for His creation, and guides each individual creature to its destiny. We should praise His name, and speak of Him in only the best and highest of terms.

The second part begins by assuring the Prophet ﷺ that although he did not know how to read, the words of the Qur'ān would be stamped on his heart and memory. Allah sent these words of comfort because in the early days of receiving the Revelation, the Prophet ﷺ was afraid that he might forget some of it. The verse 'except as Allah wills' means that he would not forget any of the Qur'ān except temporarily. Indeed, one of the miracles of the Qur'ān is that it is easy to memorize, for both Arabs

68. The *witr* prayer is a very important *sunnah* prayer which is offered at night after *ṣalāt al-'Īshā'* and before *ṣalāt al-fajr,* consisting of three *rak'ahs.* The Prophet ﷺ would often recite *al-'Alā* in the first *rak'ah,* and include *Sūrahs al-Kāfirūn, al-Ikhlāṣ, al-Falaq* or *an-Nās* in the following *rak'ahs.*

and non-Arabs, as Allah says in another *sūrah,* 'We have made the Qur'ān easy to remember' (*al-Qamar* 54: 17).[69]

The way of ease mentioned in *āyah* 8 is the *sharī'ah,* or Islamic way of life. Islam is a middle way, not a way of extremes; we neither have to perform the very difficult practices of some earlier religions, nor are we allowed to adopt the 'anything goes' attitude of modern society. In general, Allah wants things to be easy for us and not difficult. The beloved Prophet ﷺ was moderate in all of his habits, and if he had a choice between two *ḥalāl* things, he would always choose the one that was easier for people.

The rest of the *sūrah* compares the fate of the believers and unbelievers. The successful person is the one who tries to live a morally clean and pure life, devoting himself to God and not letting himself be fooled by worldly attractions. Such a person realizes that the pleasures of Paradise will be much better and everlasting. The *sūrah* ends by saying that this message to humanity is not new, but has been mentioned before in the Scriptures of the Prophets Ibrāhīm عليه السلام and Mūsā عليه السلام.

69. The Holy Qur'ān is the only religious Scripture in the world which is regularly memorized in its entirety, as has been done by children from the age of seven all over the world from the begining of Islam.

al-A'lā

[The Most High]

سُورَةُ الأَعۡلَى

In the name of Allah, the All-Merciful, the Most Kind

بِسۡمِ ٱللَّهِ ٱلرَّحۡمَٰنِ ٱلرَّحِيمِ

[1] Glorify the name of your Lord, the Most High,[70]

سَبِّحِ ٱسۡمَ رَبِّكَ ٱلۡأَعۡلَى ١

[2] Who creates, and then fashions things (in beautiful proportions),

ٱلَّذِي خَلَقَ فَسَوَّىٰ ٢

[3] Who decides (fate), and then guides (things to their destinies,

وَٱلَّذِي قَدَّرَ فَهَدَىٰ ٣

[4] Who produces the (green) pasture,

وَٱلَّذِيٓ أَخۡرَجَ ٱلۡمَرۡعَىٰ ٤

[5] and then turns it into dried, brown straw.

فَجَعَلَهُۥ غُثَآءً أَحۡوَىٰ ٥

[6] We shall make you recite so that you will not forget (O Muḥammad),

سَنُقۡرِئُكَ فَلَا تَنسَىٰٓ ٦

---

70. Here Allah commands us to say: *Subḥāna Rabbī al-A'lā* (Glory be to my Lord, the Most High) as we do while in *sujūd* in prayer.

[7] except what Allah wills. Surely He knows what is said openly and what is hidden;

إِلَّا مَا شَآءَ ٱللَّهُۚ إِنَّهُۥ يَعْلَمُ ٱلْجَهْرَ وَمَا يَخْفَىٰ ﴿٧﴾

[8] and We will ease your way to the Way of Ease (Islam).

وَنُيَسِّرُكَ لِلْيُسْرَىٰ ﴿٨﴾

[9] So (continue to) remind (people), for reminders are helpful.[71]

فَذَكِّرْ إِن نَّفَعَتِ ٱلذِّكْرَىٰ ﴿٩﴾

[10] The one who fears (God) will listen,

سَيَذَّكَّرُ مَن يَخْشَىٰ ﴿١٠﴾

[11] but the unfortunate one will avoid it,

وَيَتَجَنَّبُهَا ٱلْأَشْقَى ﴿١١﴾

[12] he who will be thrown into the great Fire

ٱلَّذِى يَصْلَى ٱلنَّارَ ٱلْكُبْرَىٰ ﴿١٢﴾

[13] where he will neither die nor live.

ثُمَّ لَا يَمُوتُ فِيهَا وَلَا يَحْيَىٰ ﴿١٣﴾

---

71. 'The Reminder' is another name for the Qur'ān itself.

[14] But successful is the one who purifies himself,[72]

قَدْ أَفْلَحَ مَن تَزَكَّىٰ ١٤

[15] and remembers the name of his Lord,[73] and prays.

وَذَكَرَ ٱسْمَ رَبِّهِۦ فَصَلَّىٰ ١٥

[16] (No), but you prefer the life of this world

بَلْ تُؤْثِرُونَ ٱلْحَيَوٰةَ ٱلدُّنْيَا ١٦

[17] even though the Next Life is better, and more lasting.

وَٱلْـَٔاخِرَةُ خَيْرٌ وَأَبْقَىٰٓ ١٧

[18] This (message) is in the earlier Scriptures –

إِنَّ هَـٰذَا لَفِى ٱلصُّحُفِ ٱلْأُولَىٰ ١٨

[19] the Books of Ibrāhīm and Mūsā.

صُحُفِ إِبْرَٰهِيمَ وَمُوسَىٰ ١٩

---

72. 'Purifies himself' or pays the purifying charity (*Zakāt*). The meaning of the word *zakāt* in Arabic is to purify, or make something clean. When we share our wealth with others, it becomes 'clean' for us to use. One explanation of this verse is that the *Zakāt* or *Ṣadaqah al-Fiṭr* (purifying charity at the end of Ramaḍān) must be paid before saying the *'Īd* prayers.

73. 'Remembers the name of his Lord', in other words by making *du'as, dhikr*, and reciting the Qur'ān regularly.

88

al-Ghāshiyah [The Overwhelming][74]

MAKKAN PERIOD

The main theme of this *sūrah* is the Resurrection, which will surprise and overwhelm people so that they feel surrounded by a catastrophe which they cannot escape. The faces of the unbelievers will appear tired and worn because they will realize that all their worldly efforts and accomplishments were useless. The believers will reach true comfort at last, in Paradise.

The next part of the *sūrah* is especially addressed to the bedouin, the Arabs of the desert who travelled through the land on camels, and had many opportunities to marvel at the vastness and wonder of Allah's creation. The unbelievers could not accept the idea of a miraculous resurrection, but isn't the fact that they could survive in the harsh desert a miracle in itself? Isn't life full of miracles all around for those who care to see?

Finally, Allah tells the Prophet ﷺ to continue reminding those around him of the message of the Qur'ān, but not to feel responsible for those who refuse to listen. It is up to Allah to deal with those who reject faith. Everyone will return to Him for the final Judgement.

74. This refers to the Judgement Day.

al-Ghāshiyah

[The Overwhelming]

سُورَةُ الغَاشِيَةِ

In the name of Allah, the All-Merciful, the Most Kind

بِسْمِ ٱللَّهِ ٱلرَّحْمَٰنِ ٱلرَّحِيمِ

[1] Has the story of the Overwhelming reached you?

هَلْ أَتَىٰكَ حَدِيثُ ٱلْغَٰشِيَةِ ١

[2] On that day (many) faces will look down (in humility)

وُجُوهٌ يَوْمَئِذٍ خَٰشِعَةٌ ٢

[3] hard-working, worn out,

عَامِلَةٌ نَّاصِبَةٌ ٣

[4] scorched by burning fire,

تَصْلَىٰ نَارًا حَامِيَةً ٤

[5] drinking from a spring of boiling water,

تُسْقَىٰ مِنْ عَيْنٍ ءَانِيَةٍ ٥

[6] no food for them except bitter cactus

لَّيْسَ لَهُمْ طَعَامٌ إِلَّا مِن ضَرِيعٍ ٦

[7] which will neither nourish them nor satisfy their hunger.

لَّا يُسْمِنُ وَلَا يُغْنِى مِن جُوعٍ ٧

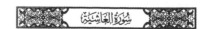

[8] On that day (other) faces will be joyful,	وُجُوهٌ يَوْمَئِذٍ نَّاعِمَةٌ ٨
[9] pleased with their past efforts,	لِّسَعْيِهَا رَاضِيَةٌ ٩
[10] in a high Garden	فِي جَنَّةٍ عَالِيَةٍ ١٠
[11] where they hear no trivial talk.[75]	لَّا تَسْمَعُ فِيهَا لَٰغِيَةً ١١
[12] In it there is a flowing fountain,	فِيهَا عَيْنٌ جَارِيَةٌ ١٢
[13] and couches raised high,	فِيهَا سُرُرٌ مَّرْفُوعَةٌ ١٣
[14] and goblets nearby,	وَأَكْوَابٌ مَّوْضُوعَةٌ ١٤
[15] and cushions arranged	وَنَمَارِقُ مَصْفُوفَةٌ ١٥
[16] and rich carpets spread around them.	وَزَرَابِيُّ مَبْثُوثَةٌ ١٦
[17] Do they not observe how the camel was created?	أَفَلَا يَنظُرُونَ إِلَى ٱلْإِبِلِ كَيْفَ خُلِقَتْ ١٧

75. 'Trivial talk' – foolish, unimportant or meaningless words; nonsense, silliness.

[18]– and the sky, how it is raised high,

وَإِلَى ٱلسَّمَآءِ كَيۡفَ رُفِعَتۡ ١٨

[19] and the mountains, how firmly they are fixed,

وَإِلَى ٱلۡجِبَالِ كَيۡفَ نُصِبَتۡ ١٩

[20] and the earth, how it is spread out?

وَإِلَى ٱلۡأَرۡضِ كَيۡفَ سُطِحَتۡ ٢٠

[21] Remind them (Muḥammad), because you were (only) sent to remind;

فَذَكِّرۡ إِنَّمَآ أَنتَ مُذَكِّرٞ ٢١

[22] you are not in charge of them.

لَّسۡتَ عَلَيۡهِم بِمُصَيۡطِرٍ ٢٢

[23] But whoever turns away and disbelieves,

إِلَّا مَن تَوَلَّىٰ وَكَفَرَ ٢٣

[24] Allah will punish him with a mighty punishment.

فَيُعَذِّبُهُ ٱللَّهُ ٱلۡعَذَابَ ٱلۡأَكۡبَرَ ٢٤

[25] Truly, they will return to Us,

إِنَّ إِلَيۡنَآ إِيَابَهُمۡ ٢٥

[26] and it is for Us to call them to account for what they have done.

ثُمَّ إِنَّ عَلَيۡنَا حِسَابَهُم ٢٦

89

al-Fajr [The Dawn]

MAKKAN PERIOD

This *sūrah* was revealed after the Makkans had begun to persecute the Muslims. It speaks to the disbelievers, reminding them of the fate of some ancient people who refused God's guidance. It also condemns their bad treatment of orphans and the poor. Beginning with an oath – about the dawn, and ten nights, and the even and odd (for which no clear explanation has come down to us in the *ḥadīth*)[76] it goes on to speak of three ancient peoples who were punished for their sins.

'Ād was an ancient tribe of southern Arabia and Iram was one of their cities; it was famous for its towering stone pillars. Allah sent the Prophet Hūd عليه السلام to the people of 'Ād, but they rejected him and were destroyed. The people of 'Ād, Thamūd and the wicked Pharaoh of Egypt are given as examples of people who were excellent engineers, proud of their beautiful and impressive buildings. Still, their great material accomplishments did not help them when Allah decided to destroy

76. Because scholars have given as many as 36 different explanations for what 'the even and the odd' might mean, we believe that a presentation of all of these ideas is too complicated and unnecessary for this book. It is one of the parts in the Qur'ān which is mystical or mysterious, and about which it is best for most people to say: 'Allah knows best its meaning.'

them for their injustice. The Prophet ﷺ warned: 'It is Allah's way that He puts down whatever raises itself up in the world.'[77]

In the third section, Allah describes those people who become proud when He showers them with riches, but complain about His treatment in times of hardship. Actually, wealth and poverty are both a test from Allah: the rich person must take care that love for his possessions does not grow in his heart, or that he becomes corrupted by money; he must remain grateful to his Lord and show his gratitude by continually sharing with the poor. On the other hand, the poor person must remain patient without complaining, or being driven to stealing or other sinful behaviour to try to improve his condition, or forgetting all of the good things he *has* been given in life. On the Last Day, everyone will be judged according to what they have been given; not only in terms of wealth, but also health, intelligence, knowledge and position. Many people will suddenly realize the true meaning of life, but sadly it will be too late.

How fortunate the soul of the believer will be on that Day, at peace with himself and his Lord – the one who remembered Allah often, fulfilled his trust, and treated his family, friends and neighbours as he liked to be treated! On that Day he will be greeted by the angels as he enters the Garden of Paradise, recognized as one who is pleased with Allah and with whom Allah is pleased.

77. *Ḥadīth* from the collection of Bukhārī.

al-Fajr

[The Dawn]

سُورَةُ الفَجۡرِ

In the name of Allah, the All-Merciful, the Most Kind

بِسۡمِ ٱللَّهِ ٱلرَّحۡمَٰنِ ٱلرَّحِيمِ

[1] By the dawn,

وَٱلۡفَجۡرِ ١

[2] and the ten nights,

وَلَيَالٍ عَشۡرٖ ٢

[3] and the even and the odd,

وَٱلشَّفۡعِ وَٱلۡوَتۡرِ ٣

[4] and the night when it passes,

وَٱلَّيۡلِ إِذَا يَسۡرِ ٤

[5] is there not an oath in this for a thinking person?

هَلۡ فِى ذَٰلِكَ قَسَمٞ لِّذِى حِجۡرٍ ٥

[6] Have you not seen how your Lord dealt with (the people of) ʿĀd?

أَلَمۡ تَرَ كَيۡفَ فَعَلَ رَبُّكَ بِعَادٍ ٦

[7] Of (the city of) Iram with towering pillars;

إِرَمَ ذَاتِ ٱلۡعِمَادِ ٧

[8] nothing like it was built in any other land.

ٱلَّتِى لَمۡ يُخۡلَقۡ مِثۡلُهَا فِى ٱلۡبِلَٰدِ ٨

[9] And with the people of Thamūd, who carved out (huge) rocks in the valley,

وَثَمُودَ ٱلَّذِينَ جَابُوا۟ ٱلصَّخْرَ بِٱلْوَادِ ﴿٩﴾

[10] and with Pharaoh of the Stakes?[78]

وَفِرْعَوْنَ ذِى ٱلْأَوْتَادِ ﴿١٠﴾

[11] They (all) rebelled (against Allah) in these lands,

ٱلَّذِينَ طَغَوْا۟ فِى ٱلْبِلَـٰدِ ﴿١١﴾

[12] and added corruption to corruption,

فَأَكْثَرُوا۟ فِيهَا ٱلْفَسَادَ ﴿١٢﴾

[13] So your Lord let loose on them a variety of punishments.

فَصَبَّ عَلَيْهِمْ رَبُّكَ سَوْطَ
عَذَابٍ ﴿١٣﴾

[14] Surely your Lord is always watching (over everything).[79]

إِنَّ رَبَّكَ لَبِٱلْمِرْصَادِ ﴿١٤﴾

---

78. Literally, 'Pharaoh, Lord of Stakes (or tent pegs)'. This phrase has been explained as referring to either the Egyptian temples with their tall columns, or by saying that this Pharaoh used to torture or kill people by putting sharp stakes through them.

79. Watching like a guard in a watchtower, or in a place where people hide, preparing for an ambush.

[15] As for man, whenever his Lord tests him by honouring and blessing him with comfort, he says (proudly), 'My Lord has honoured me!'

فَأَمَّا ٱلْإِنسَٰنُ إِذَا مَا ٱبْتَلَىٰهُ رَبُّهُۥ فَأَكْرَمَهُۥ وَنَعَّمَهُۥ فَيَقُولُ رَبِّىٓ أَكْرَمَنِ ﴿١٥﴾

[16] But when He tests him (with troubles) and limits his income, he says, 'My Lord has humiliated me.'

وَأَمَّآ إِذَا مَا ٱبْتَلَىٰهُ فَقَدَرَ عَلَيْهِ رِزْقَهُۥ فَيَقُولُ رَبِّىٓ أَهَٰنَنِ ﴿١٦﴾

[17] No, but you do not honour the orphan,

كَلَّا ۖ بَل لَّا تُكْرِمُونَ ٱلْيَتِيمَ ﴿١٧﴾

[18] and you do not urge each other to feed the poor,

وَلَا تَحَٰٓضُّونَ عَلَىٰ طَعَامِ ٱلْمِسْكِينِ ﴿١٨﴾

[19] and you greedily consume the inheritance (of the weak),[80]

وَتَأْكُلُونَ ٱلتُّرَاثَ أَكْلًا لَّمًّا ﴿١٩﴾

[20] and you are (madly) in love with money and riches!

وَتُحِبُّونَ ٱلْمَالَ حُبًّا جَمًّا ﴿٢٠﴾

---

80. This verse refers to the men who would freely use up the inheritance of orphans, women and other weak members of the family who were under their care, rather than spending it carefully.

[21] No, when the earth is ground to dust,

كَلَّآ إِذَا دُكَّتِ ٱلْأَرْضُ دَكًّا دَكًّا ﴿٢١﴾

[22] and your Lord comes, and the angels, rank after rank,

وَجَآءَ رَبُّكَ وَٱلْمَلَكُ صَفًّا صَفًّا ﴿٢٢﴾

[23] and Hell is brought near on that day. On that day, man will remember (what is important), but how will his remembering help him (then)?

وَجِاْىٓءَ يَوْمَئِذٍۭ بِجَهَنَّمَ ۚ يَوْمَئِذٍ يَتَذَكَّرُ ٱلْإِنسَٰنُ وَأَنَّىٰ لَهُ ٱلذِّكْرَىٰ ﴿٢٣﴾

[24] He will say: 'If only I had sent ahead (some good deeds) for (this) my (future) life!'

يَقُولُ يَٰلَيْتَنِى قَدَّمْتُ لِحَيَاتِى ﴿٢٤﴾

[25] On that day, no one will punish as He will punish!

فَيَوْمَئِذٍ لَّا يُعَذِّبُ عَذَابَهُۥٓ أَحَدٌ ﴿٢٥﴾

[26] And no one will bind with chains like His.

وَلَا يُوثِقُ وَثَاقَهُۥٓ أَحَدٌ ﴿٢٦﴾

[27] (But) O soul at peace!

يَٰٓأَيَّتُهَا ٱلنَّفْسُ ٱلْمُطْمَئِنَّةُ ﴿٢٧﴾

ٱرْجِعِىٓ إِلَىٰ رَبِّكِ رَاضِيَةً مَّرْضِيَّةً ﴿٢٨﴾

[28] Return to your Lord, well pleased (with Him), well pleasing.

فَٱدْخُلِى فِى عِبَٰدِى ﴿٢٩﴾

[29] Enter among My servants;

وَٱدْخُلِى جَنَّتِى ﴿٣٠﴾

[30] come into My Garden!

90

al-Balad [The City]

MAKKAN PERIOD

This *sūrah* is named after the honoured city of Makkah. Some scholars say that the parent spoken of in the first part is the Prophet Adam عليه السلام, father of the human race. Others say that it is the Prophet Ibrāhīm, father of the Jews and the Arabs through his sons Isḥāq and Ismā'īl, and the forefather of several prophets عليهم السلام ending at last with Muḥammad ﷺ. The Prophet Muḥammad ﷺ should have been respected and honoured in his own city, free to live without harm, since even the killing of animals or cutting down of trees was forbidden in Makkah before Islam, as it is today. But just as Ibrāhīm and his son عليهما السلام faced hardship thousands of years before, the Prophet Muḥammad ﷺ and his Companions endured many difficulties during the early years, and Allah states that humans were indeed created to endure hardship.

The second part of the *sūrah* describes the unbelievers who do not understand that Allah sees them, although He is the All-Seeing, the One Who created sight and gave human eyes to see with. They argue about God and boast about themselves, when it is He Who has given them their tongues and lips, to say what is good, noble and true. Allah has also shown people through His Prophets and Holy Books the two 'main roads': the steep and difficult path to goodness, and the easy path to Hell.

'Freeing a slave' is given as an example of one deed on the steep path. Although slavery is illegal and rare, there are still people who are held as captives, and others who live as slaves in a symbolic sense. Some are slaves of their selfish desires, seeking a life of unrestricted freedom and pleasure. Many become addicted to alcohol, drugs, gambling or other ills, and eventually ruin their lives and the lives of those around them. There are also poor people who live and work in miserable conditions for the rich, and people from one race or ethnic group who are oppressed by another. Helping all oppressed people is a virtue which falls under the guidance of this verse.

In this *sūrah,* believers are not described as individuals, but as members of a community of believers who help and encourage each other to be patient, and to behave well to others. People are influenced by the behaviour and values of their friends, and it is easier to unite with others to do acts of goodness than to act alone. The best Muslims are gentle, kind and supportive of each other, rather than harsh and hard-hearted. The Prophet ﷺ said: 'Show mercy to people on earth so that He who is in heaven will have mercy on you.'[81]

81. *Ḥadīth* from the collection of Tirmidhī.

al-Balad

[The City]

سُورَةُ الْبَلَدِ

In the name of Allah, the All-Merciful, the Most Kind

بِسْمِ ٱللَّهِ ٱلرَّحْمَٰنِ ٱلرَّحِيمِ

[1] No,[82] I swear by this city (of Makkah)–

لَآ أُقْسِمُ بِهَٰذَا ٱلْبَلَدِ ١

[2] and you (Muḥammad) are a free man of this city;[83]

وَأَنتَ حِلٌّۢ بِهَٰذَا ٱلْبَلَدِ ٢

[3] by the father and his children,

وَوَالِدٍ وَمَا وَلَدَ ٣

[4] surely We have created man to endure hardship.

لَقَدْ خَلَقْنَا ٱلْإِنسَٰنَ فِى كَبَدٍ ٤

[5] Does he think that no one has power over him?

أَيَحْسَبُ أَن لَّن يَقْدِرَ عَلَيْهِ أَحَدٌ ٥

---

82. When a *sūrah* begins with a 'no' followed by an oath, it was revealed in reply to something that people were saying; in other words, 'No, what you (unbelievers) are claiming is not correct; rather, it is like this ...'

83. Alternative meanings may be: (a) you are a resident in this city, and (b) the unbelievers have made your killing lawful in this city.

[6] He (boastfully) says, 'I have spent so much money on whatever I wanted.'	يَقُولُ أَهْلَكْتُ مَالًا لُّبَدًا ٦
[7] Does he think that no one sees him?	أَيَحْسَبُ أَن لَّمْ يَرَهُۥٓ أَحَدٌ ٧
[8] Have We not given him two eyes,	أَلَمْ نَجْعَل لَّهُۥ عَيْنَيْنِ ٨
[9] and a tongue and two lips,	وَلِسَانًا وَشَفَتَيْنِ ٩
[10] and shown him the two main roads (to good and evil)?	وَهَدَيْنَٰهُ ٱلنَّجْدَيْنِ ١٠
[11] But he has not tried the steep path;	فَلَا ٱقْتَحَمَ ٱلْعَقَبَةَ ١١
[12] and what will make you understand what the steep path is?	وَمَآ أَدْرَىٰكَ مَا ٱلْعَقَبَةُ ١٢
[13] It is to free a slave,	فَكُّ رَقَبَةٍ ١٣
[14] or to feed, on a day of hunger,	أَوْ إِطْعَٰمٌ فِى يَوْمٍ ذِى مَسْغَبَةٍ ١٤
[15] an orphan in the family,	يَتِيمًا ذَا مَقْرَبَةٍ ١٥

[16] or some poor man in need;[84]

أَوْ مِسْكِينًا ذَا مَتْرَبَةٍ ﴿١٦﴾

[17] and to be one of those who have faith, and encourage each other to patiently endure,[85] and encourage each other to have mercy.

ثُمَّ كَانَ مِنَ ٱلَّذِينَ ءَامَنُوا۟ وَتَوَاصَوْا۟
بِٱلصَّبْرِ وَتَوَاصَوْا۟ بِٱلْمَرْحَمَةِ ﴿١٧﴾

[18] They are the Companions of the Right Hand.[86]

أُو۟لَـٰٓئِكَ أَصْحَـٰبُ ٱلْمَيْمَنَةِ ﴿١٨﴾

[19] And as for those who do not believe in Our signs,[87] they are the Companions of the Left Hand;

وَٱلَّذِينَ كَفَرُوا۟ بِـَٔايَـٰتِنَا هُمْ
أَصْحَـٰبُ ٱلْمَشْـَٔمَةِ ﴿١٩﴾

[20] above them is a Fire, enclosed.

عَلَيْهِمْ نَارٌ مُّؤْصَدَةٌۢ ﴿٢٠﴾

---

84. Literally: 'in the dust'.

85. *Ṣabr* means endurance, or firm patience; carrying on (actively) under difficulties.

86. On the Day of Judgement, people will receive their books of the deeds they have done in their lives either in their right hand, left hand or behind their backs (see introduction to *Sūrah* 84: *al-Inshiqāq*).

87. Or 'verses'; the Arabic word *āyah* may either mean a sign, or a verse of Revelation.

91

ash-Shams [The Sun]

MAKKAN PERIOD

The first part of this *sūrah* explains that Allah has given everyone a conscience, or inner voice, to be able to know the difference between right and wrong. Whoever learns to listen to his 'good voice' will find that this voice becomes sharper and more clear; he will be successful in this life and the Next. The one who does not listen to his conscience, but follows his lower desires or the whisperings of Satan, is the one who lets his conscience become corrupted; he will be a failure.

The second part of the *sūrah* tells some of the story of the ancient Arabian tribe of Thamūd and their prophet Ṣāliḥ عليه السلام. It is said that there was not much water in the area where they lived, and that the rich and powerful tried to prevent the poor and weak from obtaining water for themselves and their cattle. As a test and punishment for their misbehaviour, Allah sent them a special, giant camel as one of His signs. He instructed the Prophet Ṣāliḥ عليه السلام to tell the people of Thamūd that they must allow this camel to graze at pasture freely and drink from the well without being disturbed for one whole day; they could graze and water their animals on the next day, and so on in turn. The people of Thamūd rebelled and disobeyed, crippling (or killing) the camel under the leadership of one especially evil man. Allah then destroyed them with an earthquake. They could have avoided this fate if they had learned to listen to the voices of their conscience.

ash-Shams

[The Sun]

سُورَةُ الشَّمۡسِ

In the name of Allah, the All-Merciful, the Most Kind

بِسۡمِ ٱللَّهِ ٱلرَّحۡمَٰنِ ٱلرَّحِيمِ

[1] By the sun and its brightness,

وَٱلشَّمۡسِ وَضُحَىٰهَا ١

[2] and the moon when it follows (it),

وَٱلۡقَمَرِ إِذَا تَلَىٰهَا ٢

[3] and the day when it displays (its brightness),

وَٱلنَّهَارِ إِذَا جَلَّىٰهَا ٣

[4] and the night when it hides it;

وَٱلَّيۡلِ إِذَا يَغۡشَىٰهَا ٤

[5] By the sky and the One Who built it,

وَٱلسَّمَآءِ وَمَا بَنَىٰهَا ٥

[6] and the earth and the One Who spread it,

وَٱلۡأَرۡضِ وَمَا طَحَىٰهَا ٦

[7] and the soul and the One Who perfected it

وَنَفۡسٖ وَمَا سَوَّىٰهَا ٧

[8] and inspired[88] it (with a conscience and knowledge of) sin and goodness:	فَأَلْهَمَهَا فُجُورَهَا وَتَقْوَىٰهَا ﴿٨﴾
[9] surely he who purifies it will succeed,	قَدْ أَفْلَحَ مَن زَكَّىٰهَا ﴿٩﴾
[10] while he who corrupts it will fail.	وَقَدْ خَابَ مَن دَسَّىٰهَا ﴿١٠﴾
[11] (The people of) Thamūd denied (their prophet) through their rebelliousness.	كَذَّبَتْ ثَمُودُ بِطَغْوَىٰهَآ ﴿١١﴾
[12] When the worst of them rushed ahead (to carry out mischief),	إِذِ ٱنۢبَعَثَ أَشْقَىٰهَا ﴿١٢﴾
[13] then Allah's messenger warned: 'This is Allah's camel, so let her drink!'	فَقَالَ لَهُمْ رَسُولُ ٱللَّهِ نَاقَةَ ٱللَّهِ وَسُقْيَـٰهَا ﴿١٣﴾

88. In this sentence, 'inspired' means gave it spiritual guidance.

[14] But they rejected him and hamstrung[98] her, so their Lord crushed them for their sin and levelled them (to the ground),

فَكَذَّبُوهُ فَعَقَرُوهَا فَدَمْدَمَ عَلَيْهِمْ
رَبُّهُم بِذَنۢبِهِمْ فَسَوَّىٰهَا ﴿١٤﴾

[15] and He does not fear the consequences.[90]

وَلَا يَخَافُ عُقْبَٰهَا ﴿١٥﴾

---

89. The hamstrings are the main tendons at the back of the knee which allow a person's or animal's leg to move; 'to hamstring' means to cut these tendons so that the animal will be crippled and unable to graze for food. Another meaning of *'aqarūhā* is 'they killed her'.

90. In other words, Allah is All-Powerful and is not afraid of destroying evil people. No one can 'take revenge' on Him. Some scholars say that 'he' refers to the leader of the evil people of Thamūd.

92

al-Layl [The Night]

MAKKAN PERIOD

This *sūrah* begins with a comparison between the opposites of night and day, and male and female, to introduce its main theme: the difference between people who are generous and good, and those who are greedy and badly behaved. It is true that people come in many degrees of goodness or evil; there is no person so bad that he has no good in him at all, and there is no person so good that he cannot improve himself. Still, humans can be divided generally into two groups: just as the male is distinct from the female, and night from day, so are good people clearly different from bad.

Some people believe that there is no real good or evil; they say that what is good for one person may be bad for someone else, or what was important yesterday may not be important tomorrow. People who think this way say that everything is 'relative', so everyone must decide what to do for themselves. For everything which people normally think of as bad, someone can come up with an excuse as to why it really might be good. Such arguments come from not having a criterion for Judgement – a clear way to decide about something.

Allah has revealed the Qur'ān as *al-Furqān*, the main

criterion of judging good and evil. It is a comprehensive book which teaches us not only what we should believe but also how we should behave, and its rules do not change with time. Everyone who accepts that there is One God and that Muḥammad ﷺ is His Last Messenger should try to follow its guidance as best he can. He should also follow the beautiful example of the Prophet Muḥammad ﷺ who was sent as a mercy to humanity.

Whenever Allah sent a holy Scripture to a group of people, He sent it through a Prophet. Why didn't Allah just send a book on a mountain top, delivered by angels? Because people can misunderstand a book, and it is more difficult to learn from a book than from a teacher. People learn best by imitating and following other people; books help us to remember what we have learned. Even the Prophet ﷺ learned the Qur'ān and some other things from the Angel Jibrā'īl عليه السلام, who often came to him in human form. So Allah, Who understands human nature better than anyone, and Who cares more than anyone that we will learn our lessons and remember them, sent us His beloved Messenger along with His Glorious Qur'ān as a teacher. Then the Prophet's Companions رضي الله عنه learned from the Prophet ﷺ, and the later generations learned from them, and so it continues.

We should do our best to study the Qur'ān and the Traditions of the Prophet ﷺ under the guidance of honest and reliable *imāms*, *shaykhs* and *'ulamā'* (religious scholars) who have studied the Arabic language, the biography of the Prophet ﷺ, the lives of the *Ṣaḥābah* رضي الله عنه, and other religious knowledge in order to help Muslims to better understand what Allah wants of us. A person who has not studied Islam in depth cannot be sure that he will arrive at the correct conclusion simply by reading the Qur'ān and *Ḥadīth*, especially when using a translation rather than the original Arabic, or when dealing with a complicated question or problem. He should take the safe course of action by seeking the advice of someone with more knowledge than himself. In case he does not receive clear advice or cannot find an answer in time, he can consult his heart. When asked about righteous conduct, the Prophet ﷺ said: 'Righteousness is good character, and sin is what makes you uncomfortable inside, and you would not like other people to find out about.'[91]

If a person becomes aware of the right thing to do but continues to do what is wrong, then Allah will 'ease his way to hardship' (*āyah* 10). In the opinion of some scholars, this means not only that he will be punished in Hell, but that it will become easier for him to do more bad deeds that will lead him to Hell. If a person does not listen to his conscience it becomes 'rusty', and after some time it will not raise objections to anything he does. For instance, a child who tells lies regularly will become more and more used to lying until he cannot stop himself; when he grows up, he may not even be able to tell the difference between his own lie and the truth. On the other hand, a person who gets into the habit of doing good will find it harder and harder to do anything else; Allah will 'ease his way' to performing more good deeds, and to comfort in the next life.

91. *Ḥadīth* from the collection of Muslim.

There are some people who claim to be believers but are not sincere; they pray in front of others, not out of fear and love of Allah, but in the hope that people will notice them. They may give a lot to charity so that people will say that they are generous. Such actions will not be accepted by Allah on the Last Day. The only good deeds that are truly acceptable are those which are done 'without any thought of reward' (*āyah* 19) except the great hope and desire to earn Allah's pleasure and live in His Presence in *Jannah* (Garden of Paradise).[92]

92. The Prophet ﷺ explained: 'Actions will be judged according to the intentions behind them', in a *ḥadīth* which is considered to be so important that it is placed at the beginning of many *ḥadīth* collections.

al-Layl

سُورَةُ اللَّيْلِ

[The Night]

In the name of Allah, the All-Merciful, the Most Kind

بِسْمِ ٱللَّهِ ٱلرَّحْمَٰنِ ٱلرَّحِيمِ

[1] By the night when it veils (with darkness),

وَٱلَّيْلِ إِذَا يَغْشَىٰ ﴿١﴾

[2] and the day when it shines brightly,

وَٱلنَّهَارِ إِذَا تَجَلَّىٰ ﴿٢﴾

[3] and the One Who created the male and female,

وَمَا خَلَقَ ٱلذَّكَرَ وَٱلْأُنثَىٰٓ ﴿٣﴾

[4] surely your efforts are directed towards different goals.

إِنَّ سَعْيَكُمْ لَشَتَّىٰ ﴿٤﴾

[5] As for the one who gives (in charity) and fears Allah,

فَأَمَّا مَنْ أَعْطَىٰ وَٱتَّقَىٰ ﴿٥﴾

[6] and is a truthful witness to (His) goodness,[93]

وَصَدَّقَ بِٱلْحُسْنَىٰ ﴿٦﴾

---

93. According to many scholars, this means to bear witness that 'there is no god but Allah (the One God).'

[7] We will ease his way to comfort (in the Next Life).	فَسَنُيَسِّرُهُۥ لِلْيُسْرَىٰ ٧
[8] But as for the stingy one who thinks he needs no one,	وَأَمَّا مَنۢ بَخِلَ وَٱسْتَغْنَىٰ ٨
[9] and lies about (Allah's) goodness,	وَكَذَّبَ بِٱلْحُسْنَىٰ ٩
[10] We will ease his way to hardship.	فَسَنُيَسِّرُهُۥ لِلْعُسْرَىٰ ١٠
[11] His wealth will not save him when he perishes (in the Fire).	وَمَا يُغْنِى عَنْهُ مَالُهُۥٓ إِذَا تَرَدَّىٰٓ ١١
[12] Surely it is for Us to give guidance,	إِنَّ عَلَيْنَا لَلْهُدَىٰ ١٢
[13] and surely to Us belong the end and the beginning (of all things).	وَإِنَّ لَنَا لَلْءَاخِرَةَ وَٱلْأُولَىٰ ١٣

[14] So I warn you of a blazing Fire;

فَأَنذَرْتُكُمْ نَارًا تَلَظَّىٰ ﴿١٤﴾

[15] none but the most miserable will enter it –

لَا يَصْلَىٰهَآ إِلَّا ٱلْأَشْقَى ﴿١٥﴾

[16] he who denies the Truth and turns his back.

ٱلَّذِى كَذَّبَ وَتَوَلَّىٰ ﴿١٦﴾

[17] But the most righteous will be taken far away from it –

وَسَيُجَنَّبُهَا ٱلْأَتْقَى ﴿١٧﴾

[18] he who gives away his wealth to purify himself,

ٱلَّذِى يُؤْتِى مَالَهُۥ يَتَزَكَّىٰ ﴿١٨﴾

[19] without thought of reward or favour,

وَمَا لِأَحَدٍ عِندَهُۥ مِن نِّعْمَةٍ تُجْزَىٰٓ ﴿١٩﴾

[20] but only the desire to see the Face of his Lord Most High;[94]

إِلَّا ٱبْتِغَآءَ وَجْهِ رَبِّهِ ٱلْأَعْلَىٰ ﴿٢٠﴾

---

94. Or, 'but only the desire for his Lord's good pleasure'. One of the rewards of the people of Paradise will be to see Allah's Face and be in His Presence, as confirmed by the following *aḥādīth*: 'When the inhabitants of Paradise have entered Paradise, Allah, the Blessed and Exalted, (*Continued on page 111*)

[21] he will surely reach complete satisfaction.

وَلَسَوْفَ يَرْضَىٰ ﴿٢١﴾

(*Continued from page 110*)

will ask them: "Do you desire anything that I should give you?" They will answer: "Have You not brightened our faces? Have You not admitted us to Paradise and saved us from the Fire?" Then, Allah will lift the veil from His Face and the people of Paradise will not have known anything more precious than looking at their Lord' (Muslim), and 'You will surely see your Lord just as you are seeing this (full) moon, without any disturbance' (Bukhārī and Muslim).

There are eleven verses of the Qur'ān in which Allah's Face is mentioned, and other verses which mention His Hands and other body parts. Still, we should not misunderstand that Allah has a body like a human, because He is unlike anything in His creation. He knows best what He means by 'His Face' or 'His Hands'. We can understand this verse to mean that Allah will allow the believers to draw near to Him: they will be extremely happy and satisfied, in the way that someone might feel very honoured to sit in the presence of a king or president and be able to speak to him face-to-face, only much more so.

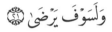

93

aḍ-Ḍuḥā [The Morning Light]

MAKKAN PERIOD

This *sūrah* was revealed in the early days of the Prophet's mission ﷺ during a period when the angel had not come with any new revelations for some time. The unbelievers of Makkah started to tease the Prophet ﷺ, saying that his 'devil' had abandoned him. So, the first section begins by assuring him that Allah certainly had not abandoned him, and that everything would turn out well in the end.

The second section reminds the Prophet ﷺ that Allah had helped him out of many troubles before. The beloved Messenger of Allah ﷺ had been distressed by the death of his father, mother and grandfather in his early childhood; Allah provided for him through the care of his uncle and later through his marriage to his first wife, Khadījah ؓ, who was a wealthy woman. From a difficult beginning Allah raised him to a position of fame, at first because of his honesty and good character and later through his mission to humanity.

It often happens that people with humble beginnings become corrupted when they rise to high positions of power or fame. Many wealthy businessmen who began their careers as poor shoe-shiners on the street or newspaper boys forget their simple origins after they join the rich crowd. They begin to look down on people whom they think are 'lower' than themselves, and treat them badly. This attitude comes from their thinking that they have made their own success, not realizing that they could never have achieved anything without the support and grace of Allah.

This *sūrah* was revealed before the Prophet's mission became successful, but Allah instructed him and all of the believers in advance to be very careful of their treatment of those more unfortunate than themselves. The blessed Prophet ﷺ was the best example when it came to treating people well. Even during his busiest period in Madīnah he would always take time to personally attend to the needs of women and children, and the weak and poor. He remained humble even when he was the leader of all Arabia, and his own family often went without food so that others could eat.

All of us face problems from day to day, but we should never forget Allah's kindness. Rather than comparing our lives with those of other people who have more than we do, we should compare our lives with those millions of people who have less, and be grateful. Even if we live in an area where we never see a really poor person or ever know an orphan, still there are always things we can do to help others less fortunate than ourselves.

aḍ-Ḍuḥā

[The Morning Light]

سُورَةُ الضُّحَىٰ

In the name of Allah, the All-Merciful, the Most Kind

بِسۡمِ ٱللَّهِ ٱلرَّحۡمَٰنِ ٱلرَّحِيمِ

[1] By the morning brightness,

وَٱلضُّحَىٰ ١

[2] and by the night when all is still,

وَٱلَّيۡلِ إِذَا سَجَىٰ ٢

[3] your Lord has not forgotten you, nor is He displeased,

مَا وَدَّعَكَ رَبُّكَ وَمَا قَلَىٰ ٣

[4] and the time to come will be better than the past![95]

وَلَلۡأٓخِرَةُ خَيۡرٞ لَّكَ مِنَ ٱلۡأُولَىٰ ٤

[5] Soon your Lord will give to you, and you will be satisfied.

وَلَسَوۡفَ يُعۡطِيكَ رَبُّكَ فَتَرۡضَىٰٓ ٥

[6] Did He not find you as an orphan and give you shelter?

أَلَمۡ يَجِدۡكَ يَتِيمٗا فَـَٔاوَىٰ ٦

---

95. Or, 'the next life will be better for you than this one'.

[7] Did He not find you lost, and guide you?[96]

وَوَجَدَكَ ضَآلًّا فَهَدَىٰ ﴿٧﴾

[8] Did He not find you in need, and enrich you?

وَوَجَدَكَ عَآئِلًا فَأَغْنَىٰ ﴿٨﴾

[9] So, as for the orphan, do not oppress him;

فَأَمَّا ٱلْيَتِيمَ فَلَا تَقْهَرْ ﴿٩﴾

[10] and the beggar, do not send him away (empty-handed);

وَأَمَّا ٱلسَّآئِلَ فَلَا تَنْهَرْ ﴿١٠﴾

[11] and as for your Lord's beautiful gifts, declare them (to others).

وَأَمَّا بِنِعْمَةِ رَبِّكَ فَحَدِّثْ ﴿١١﴾

---

96. The Prophet ﷺ never worshipped idols as a child or young person, although almost everyone around him did; but still he was without true guidance in religion, and therefore 'lost' until Allah revealed to him the Straight Path.

94

al-Inshirāḥ [The Expansion]

MAKKAN PERIOD

This *sūrah* was revealed in the very early days of the Prophet's mission, soon after the previous *sūrah, aḍ-Ḍuḥā,* and is very similar to it in style and subject matter. The Prophet ﷺ had been very troubled in his early years by the terrible things that went on in Makkan society: baby girls were buried alive because their parents did not want to pay to feed and clothe them; poor people were exploited or abused by the rich; families continued blood-feuds for generations, killing innocent people and continuing hatreds. In place of the simple and pure worship of One God, established by their great forefather Ibrāhīm عليه السلام, the Arabs worshipped any of the 360 idols that were standing around the Kaʿbah, either alone or as 'intermediaries' between themselves and Allah, the great God. All of these things greatly disturbed the young Muḥammad ﷺ, who instinctively felt how wrong everything was around him. When the Angel Jibrā'īl عليه السلام came to him with Allah's Word, it was a great source of comfort, an 'opening' of his heart and easing of his burden.

After reminding the Prophet ﷺ of Allah's great favours granted to him, the *sūrah* goes on to say that Allah always sends some relief along with every difficulty.

The final verses can be understood to mean that we should continue to strive to perform our worship even after Allah has eased our load, since many people pray when they are in trouble, but forget Allah when everything is going well. It can also mean that we should make good use of our free time once we are done with our work. When we have taken care of our worldly responsibility, we should spend part of the evening and night hours with our Lord, in worship.[97]

97. The Prophet ﷺ and his close Companions ؓ used to spend two or more hours each night in *ṣalāh, du'ā', dhikr,* and reciting the Qur'ān. *Ṣalāt at-tahajjud,* a voluntary prayer offered in the last hours of the night before *fajr,* is associated with many blessings.

al-Inshirāḥ

[The Expansion]

سُورَةُ الشَّرۡحِ

In the name of Allah, the All-Merciful, the Most Kind

بِسۡمِ ٱللَّهِ ٱلرَّحۡمَٰنِ ٱلرَّحِيمِ

[1] Have We not expanded your breast[98]

أَلَمۡ نَشۡرَحۡ لَكَ صَدۡرَكَ ١

[2] and lifted off your burden

وَوَضَعۡنَا عَنكَ وِزۡرَكَ ٢

[3] which had weighed down your back?

ٱلَّذِيٓ أَنقَضَ ظَهۡرَكَ ٣

[4] And (have We not) exalted your fame?[99]

وَرَفَعۡنَا لَكَ ذِكۡرَكَ ٤

---

98. Some scholars say that this verse refers to an incident in the life of the Prophet ﷺ when he was a young boy living with Ḥalīmah, his wet-nurse and foster mother. He used to go out in the desert with the other children to watch the sheep. One day two angels came to him, laid him down gently, opened his chest without hurting him in any way, and removed a black spot from his heart, which is a symbol of all evil. Then they closed his chest, told him to always be kind and merciful to others, and left him to play with his friends, who had been watching fearfully from a distance. His playmates reported what had happened to Ḥalīmah, who reported it to Āminah, Muḥammad's mother.

99. Since this verse was revealed in the very early days of Islam before the Prophet ﷺ actually became famous, it was a prophecy of the future. Muḥammad ﷺ was the first prophet we know of who achieved

(*Continued on page 119*)

[5] So, surely, with hardship comes ease,

فَإِنَّ مَعَ ٱلْعُسْرِ يُسْرًا ٥

[6] surely, with hardship comes ease.

إِنَّ مَعَ ٱلْعُسْرِ يُسْرًا ٦

[7] So whenever you are free (from your duties), continue to work

فَإِذَا فَرَغْتَ فَٱنصَبْ ٧

[8] and turn all your attention to your Lord.

وَإِلَىٰ رَبِّكَ فَٱرْغَب ٨

(*Continued from page 118*)
such extraordinary success: by the time of his death, the entire Arabian peninsula was united under the banner of Islam. When the Prophet ﷺ was born, his very name was rare or unknown among Arabs. Now, fourteen hundred years later, the name 'Muḥammad' and its derivatives (Aḥmad, Ḥamīd, Maḥmūd, etc.) is the most popular boy's name in the world. There is no moment in which the blessed Prophet ﷺ is not mentioned somewhere in the world – whether in someone declaring the *shahādah,* calling the *adhān,* performing the *ṣalāh,* giving the *khuṭbah,* or making *du'ā'.* This is Allah's special favour to him ﷺ as His final Messenger and beloved servant.

95

at-Tīn [The Fig]

MAKKAN PERIOD

This *sūrah* begins with an oath which has been explained in several different ways by Qur'ānic scholars. One is that each item in the oath represents a different period in the history of humankind, and the major prophets of those times.

1. The fig stands for the period of the first humans and the Prophet Adam ﷺ, because it is said that he and his wife covered themselves with fig leaves in the Garden of Paradise.
2. The olive symbolises the period after the Flood and the Prophet Nūḥ ﷺ, because it is said that he sent a dove out of the Ark to find dry land and it came back with an olive leaf.
3. Mount Sinai is a symbol of the Prophet Mūsā ﷺ and the beginning of the Jewish law, because that is the mountain where he received his Revelation.
4. 'This city of safety' refers to Makkah and the blessed Prophet Muḥammad ﷺ, whose period of prophethood shall last until the Last Day.[100]

100. Other explanations include:

- that 'the fig and the olive' refer to the major source of these fruits – Palestine and Syria – lands which were also the birthplace of several prophets.
- that 'the olive' stands for the Mount of Olives in Jerusalem where Jesus ﷺ received his Revelation.

Allah then goes on to say that He created humans in the best of forms, and then reduced them to the lowest of the low – except those who believe and do good. What does this mean? Humans are the height of creation, in that God blew something of His own Spirit into the humble form of clay from which Adam ﷺ was made. Allah honoured Adam ﷺ and his children above other creatures, giving humans the possibility of reaching a rank as high as the angels', through obedience.[101] On the other hand, people who ignore their higher nature can come down to a level of behaviour much worse than the most savage animals. Lions and other beasts of prey only kill because of hunger, as needed; people are capable of inflicting the most terrible torture and inhumane treatment on each other because of political ideas, religious intolerance or ethnic hatred. People are always inventing new weapons to cause more pain or destruction, who find new ways of causing suffering to others. Is that not truly 'the lowest of the low'?

The *sūrah* ends by asking what could make people deny the final Judgement? After all, many of the worst criminals are never caught or punished during their lives on earth, and many people who do their best throughout their lives are never rewarded. We expect earthly judges

101. Angels were created without personal will as obedient servants of Allah; they cannot disobey His orders, so they do not have the same rank as humans who can choose to sin but remain obedient, like prophets and their sincere followers.

to punish those murderers, drug-dealers, thieves, and other criminals who harm innocent people; shall not Allah hand out exact justice to His creatures one day?

at-Tin

[The Fig]

سُورَةُ التِّينِ

In the name of Allah, the All-Merciful, the Most Kind

بِسْمِ ٱللَّهِ ٱلرَّحْمَٰنِ ٱلرَّحِيمِ

[1] By the fig and the olive,

وَٱلتِّينِ وَٱلزَّيْتُونِ ﴿١﴾

[2] and Mount Sinai,

وَطُورِ سِينِينَ ﴿٢﴾

[3] and this city, a safe haven,

وَهَٰذَا ٱلْبَلَدِ ٱلْأَمِينِ ﴿٣﴾

[4] Surely We made man in the best of forms,

لَقَدْ خَلَقْنَا ٱلْإِنسَٰنَ فِىٓ أَحْسَنِ
تَقْوِيمٍ ﴿٤﴾

[5] then We reduced him to the lowest of the low,

ثُمَّ رَدَدْنَٰهُ أَسْفَلَ سَٰفِلِينَ ﴿٥﴾

[6] except for those who believe and do good deeds: they shall have a never-ending reward.

إِلَّا ٱلَّذِينَ ءَامَنُوا۟ وَعَمِلُوا۟
ٱلصَّٰلِحَٰتِ فَلَهُمْ أَجْرٌ غَيْرُ
مَمْنُونٍ ﴿٦﴾

فَمَا يُكَذِّبُكَ بَعْدُ بِٱلدِّينِ ﴿٧﴾

[7] What then, after this, can make you deny the Judgement?

أَلَيْسَ ٱللَّهُ بِأَحْكَمِ ٱلْحَٰكِمِينَ ﴿٨﴾

[8] Is Allah not the wisest of Judges?

96

al-ʿAlaq [The Clot]

MAKKAN PERIOD

The first five verses of this *sūrah* were the first revelation of the Qur'ān. The Angel Jibrā'īl ﷺ came to the Prophet Muḥammad ﷺ when he was on a spiritual retreat in a cave outside Makkah, at the age of 40. The angel commanded him to read, and the Prophet ﷺ answered that he did not know how to read. Then the angel squeezed him and said again, 'Read!', and the Prophet ﷺ again answered that he did not know how to read. Finally, when the Angel Jibrā'īl ﷺ squeezed him very hard and ordered him for a third time to read, the Prophet ﷺ asked, 'What shall I read?', and Jibrā'īl ﷺ answered, 'Read in the name of your Lord ...' It seemed to the Prophet ﷺ that these words were etched in his memory. The angel went out of the cave, and the Prophet Muḥammad ﷺ saw Jibrā'īl's ﷺ shape fill the entire horizon. He then told him, 'I am the Angel Jibrā'īl, and you, Muḥammad, are the Messenger of Allah.' This beautiful story can be read in more detail in books of *sīrah.*

The second part of the *sūrah* was revealed after the beloved Messenger of Allah ﷺ was threatened by one of his main enemies, Abū Jahl. Before the Prophet ﷺ even began to preach Islam openly, he went to the Kaʿbah and prayed as Allah had taught him. The people of the Quraysh were curious, as they could see that this new practice meant that he must have adopted some new religion. Abū Jahl, rather than waiting to ask what the prayer was all about, immediately began to ridicule the Prophet ﷺ and said that if he caught Muḥammad with his face on the ground, he would step on his neck and rub his face in the dust! When the Prophet ﷺ heard about his remark he said: 'If he did that, the angels would grab him right then and there.'[102]

One of the most important lessons to be learned from this *sūrah* is the high value attached to reading and knowledge in Islam. In the days before Islam (called the *Jāhiliyyah* or 'Days of Ignorance') most people did not know how to read. Learning was a privilege for the rich upper classes, or for priests. The command to read was the first revelation the Prophet ﷺ received.[103] Later, when the Muslims were forced to fight to defend themselves, he freed any captive who could teach ten Muslims to read. Islam is the first religion to encourage *all* of its followers to read, and to study and learn as much as they can. At a time when women of almost all religions and cultures were not allowed to study, the Prophet ﷺ said: 'The search for knowledge is a duty for every Muslim, male and female.'

Because early Muslims considered that learning was a way to worship Allah and earn His pleasure, they began

102. *Ḥadīth* recorded by Bukhārī, Tirmidhī, Nasā'ī and others.

103. *Iqra'* means 'to read out loud', or 'recite' in the Arabic language (silent reading was uncommon at that time); *Qur'ān* means 'that which is read (out loud)' or 'The Recital'.

to discover, invent and create many, many new things which changed human life on earth in every area: science, medicine, engineering, architecture, art, government and more. The first universities and public hospitals in the world were established by Muslims more than a thousand years ago, free to anyone who needed them. The story of the early Muslims and their achievements may be discovered in specialized history books; it is exciting and full of surprises.[104]

Why is knowledge so important? Knowledge feeds our minds and spirits, just as food feeds our bodies. The human ability to learn is one of Allah's great mercies to us, and one of the ways He has honoured us above the rest of His creatures. From the thrill of first learning how to walk or talk or tie our shoelaces, we continue to learn every day of our lives until we die. Knowledge is a comfort to the believer, a source of wisdom and guidance and a means to happiness.

Allah says in this *sūrah* that He teaches us 'by the Pen' what we did not know. The most important knowledge is that which we can learn from the Qur'ān and other religious writings on how to live; after religious knowledge, in importance comes any knowledge which is helpful for ourselves and others in society, animals, and the earth we are guardians of. Knowledge is unlimited; it never ends. In the words of the Qur'ān: 'Above every knower there is One All-Knowing' (*Yūsuf* 12: 76), and Allah is the Knower of all. We should ask, as Allah has taught us to, 'O Lord, increase me in knowledge' (*Ṭā Hā* 20: 114).

---

104. See Bibliography for a list of recommended reading.

al-'Alaq

[The Clot]

سُورَةُ العَلَق

In the name of Allah, the All-Merciful, the Most Kind

بِسۡمِ ٱللَّهِ ٱلرَّحۡمَٰنِ ٱلرَّحِيمِ

[1] Read! in the name of your Lord Who created;

ٱقۡرَأۡ بِٱسۡمِ رَبِّكَ ٱلَّذِي خَلَقَ ١

[2] created man from a (tiny) clot, clinging (to its mother).[105]

خَلَقَ ٱلۡإِنسَٰنَ مِنۡ عَلَقٍ ٢

[3] Read! And your Lord is Most Generous,

ٱقۡرَأۡ وَرَبُّكَ ٱلۡأَكۡرَمُ ٣

[4] Who taught by the Pen;

ٱلَّذِي عَلَّمَ بِٱلۡقَلَمِ ٤

[5] taught man what he did not know.

عَلَّمَ ٱلۡإِنسَٰنَ مَا لَمۡ يَعۡلَمۡ ٥

---

105. Babies first start growing from tiny fertilized eggs, which look like clots of blood very early in their development. They cling to the insides of their mothers in the way that tiny seeds hold to the earth by their roots, growing stage by stage from embryo to foetus to newborn infant. This is one of the great miracles of Allah's creation. (For an explanation of the Arabic word *'alaq* as meaning 'something which clings', refer to *The Bible, the Qur'ān and Science* by Maurice Bucaille.)

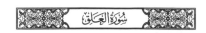

[6] No, but truly man is arrogant;

كَلَّآ إِنَّ ٱلْإِنسَٰنَ لَيَطْغَىٰٓ ٦

[7] he thinks that he needs no help (from Allah).

أَن رَّءَاهُ ٱسْتَغْنَىٰٓ ٧

[8] Surely the return (of all things) is to Allah.

إِنَّ إِلَىٰ رَبِّكَ ٱلرُّجْعَىٰٓ ٨

[9] Have you seen the one who prevents

أَرَءَيْتَ ٱلَّذِى يَنْهَىٰ ٩

[10] a servant (of Allah) from praying?[106]

عَبْدًا إِذَا صَلَّىٰٓ ١٠

[11] Have you considered whether he is following guidance,

أَرَءَيْتَ إِن كَانَ عَلَى ٱلْهُدَىٰٓ ١١

[12] or encourages righteousness?

أَوْ أَمَرَ بِٱلتَّقْوَىٰٓ ١٢

[13] Have you considered: what if he denies (the truth) and turns away?

أَرَءَيْتَ إِن كَذَّبَ وَتَوَلَّىٰٓ ١٣

---

106. This verse and the ones which follow were revealed because of Abū Jahl, who did everything he could to prevent people from practising Islam. However, they can apply to anyone.

[14] Does he not know that Allah sees (him)?

أَلَمْ يَعْلَم بِأَنَّ ٱللَّهَ يَرَىٰ ﴿١٤﴾

[15] No, surely, if he does not stop We will grab him by his forelock;

كَلَّا لَئِن لَّمْ يَنتَهِ لَنَسْفَعًۢا بِٱلنَّاصِيَةِ ﴿١٥﴾

[16] a lying, sinful forelock;

نَاصِيَةٍ كَـٰذِبَةٍ خَاطِئَةٍ ﴿١٦﴾

[17] then let him call his friends and protectors (as if they could help)!

فَلْيَدْعُ نَادِيَهُۥ ﴿١٧﴾

[18] We will call the angels of punishment (to deal with him)!

سَنَدْعُ ٱلزَّبَانِيَةَ ﴿١٨﴾

[19] No! Do not obey him, but prostrate yourself and draw near (to Allah).[107]

كَلَّا لَا تُطِعْهُ وَٱسْجُدْ
وَٱقْتَرِب ۩ ﴿١٩﴾

---

107. This is one of the special *'sajdah'* verses in the Qur'ān; anyone who recites it in Arabic or hears it recited by someone else should prostrate himself on the ground as we do in prayer. The Prophet ﷺ said that a person is closest to Allah when prostrating before his Lord, in *sajdah*. (*Ḥadīth* from the collection of Bukhārī.)

97

al-Qadr [The Power]

MAKKAN PERIOD

Laylat al-Qadr, or the Night of Power, is the anniversary of the night that the Qur'ān was sent down from the Preserved Tablet to the lowest of the seven heavens. It is also the night that the Angel Jibrā'īl ﷺ appeared to the Prophet ﷺ in the cave with the first revelation of the Qur'ān (*al-'Alaq* 96: 1-5). Allah created seven heavens or 'layers of space', and according to *ḥadīth,* the entire Qur'ān came down at once to the lowest heaven, from the Preserved Tablet where everything that will happen from the beginning of time until the Last Day is written.

The Night of Power falls on one of the odd-numbered nights of the last ten days of the month of Ramaḍān (the 21st, 23rd, 25th, 27th or 29th). During these last ten days the Prophet ﷺ and his Companions ﷺ used to stay in the mosque in seclusion (*I'tikāf*), praying and reading the Qur'ān, and waiting for this special night on which the angels come down to earth with Allah's commands. It is said that if a person is awake on this night and asks Allah for something, He will grant his prayer. It is a time of great peace and satisfaction. Why doesn't Allah tell us exactly which night it is? Perhaps He wants us to make effort for it; people appreciate things more when they have to struggle to obtain them.

al-Qadr

[The Power]

سُورَةُ الْقَدْرِ

In the name of Allah, the All-Merciful, the Most Kind

بِسْمِ ٱللَّهِ ٱلرَّحْمَٰنِ ٱلرَّحِيمِ

[1] Surely We sent it down on the Night of Power.

إِنَّآ أَنزَلْنَٰهُ فِى لَيْلَةِ ٱلْقَدْرِ ﴿١﴾

[2] And what can make you understand what the Night of Power is?

وَمَآ أَدْرَىٰكَ مَا لَيْلَةُ ٱلْقَدْرِ ﴿٢﴾

[3] The Night of Power is better than a thousand months!

لَيْلَةُ ٱلْقَدْرِ خَيْرٌ مِّنْ أَلْفِ شَهْرٍ ﴿٣﴾

[4] In it the angels and the Spirit[108] come down by the permission of their Lord, with all (His) commands (for the coming year).

تَنَزَّلُ ٱلْمَلَٰٓئِكَةُ وَٱلرُّوحُ فِيهَا بِإِذْنِ
رَبِّهِم مِّن كُلِّ أَمْرٍ ﴿٤﴾

[5] It is Peace! ... until the break of dawn.

سَلَٰمٌ هِىَ حَتَّىٰ مَطْلَعِ ٱلْفَجْرِ ﴿٥﴾

---

108. According to most scholars, 'the Spirit' here means the Angel Jibrā'īl عليه السلام.

98

al-Bayyinah [The Clear Proof]

MADĪNAN PERIOD

This *sūrah* describes the difference between true believers and unbelievers. The 'Clear Proof' is the Qur'ān and the *Sunnah*: the Prophet Muḥammad ﷺ is the Messenger of Allah who is mentioned, and the pure pages are those of the Qur'ān. The term 'People of the Book' is used in the Qur'ān to mean Christians and Jews, who have been given Divinely revealed books of Scripture: the Torah to the Jews and the *Injīl*, or Gospel, to the Christians. Allah says that some of them are true believers, but most are not.

Idol-worshippers and those People of the Book who had become confused could never have found a way out of their mistaken beliefs until Allah sent His Messenger Muḥammad ﷺ with the Qur'ān, to explain the issues that had confused them. But not all of the People of the Book in Arabia and surrounding lands accepted the Qur'ān and the beloved Prophet ﷺ. They became divided into small sects, arguing with each other about minor details. Allah presents here the essence of true religion: to serve only Him as the One True God with a sincere heart, pray regularly and share whatever one has with others.

Those who reject the truth after it has been clearly explained to them are among the worst of creation, and are destined for punishment. Those who struggle with themselves to remain faithfully obedient to Allah's laws are among the best of creation; unlike the angels, they have been given a free will to do good or bad, and they earn Allah's pleasure through their good choices.

al-Bayyinah

[The Clear Proof]

سُورَةُ البَيِّنَةِ

In the name of Allah, the All-Merciful, the Most Kind

بِسْمِ ٱللَّهِ ٱلرَّحْمَٰنِ ٱلرَّحِيمِ

[1] Those People of the Book who are unbelievers, and the idol-worshippers, could never have left (their mistaken beliefs) until the Clear Proof came to them:

لَمْ يَكُنِ ٱلَّذِينَ كَفَرُوا۟ مِنْ أَهْلِ
ٱلْكِتَٰبِ وَٱلْمُشْرِكِينَ مُنفَكِّينَ
حَتَّىٰ تَأْتِيَهُمُ ٱلْبَيِّنَةُ ﴿١﴾

[2] a Messenger from Allah, reciting pure pages

رَسُولٌ مِّنَ ٱللَّهِ يَتْلُوا۟ صُحُفًا مُّطَهَّرَةً ﴿٢﴾

[3] with correct Scriptures.

فِيهَا كُتُبٌ قَيِّمَةٌ ﴿٣﴾

[4] And the People of the Book did not divide into sects until the Clear Proof came to them;

وَمَا تَفَرَّقَ ٱلَّذِينَ أُوتُوا۟ ٱلْكِتَٰبَ
إِلَّا مِنۢ بَعْدِ مَا جَآءَتْهُمُ ٱلْبَيِّنَةُ ﴿٤﴾

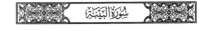

[5] Though they were not ordered to do anything except to serve Allah, devoting themselves sincerely to Him alone, true and faithful, and to establish the prayers, and pay the *Zakāt* (purifying alms).[109] That is the true religion.[110]

وَمَآ أُمِرُوٓاْ إِلَّا لِيَعۡبُدُواْ ٱللَّهَ مُخۡلِصِينَ لَهُ ٱلدِّينَ حُنَفَآءَ وَيُقِيمُواْ ٱلصَّلَوٰةَ وَيُؤۡتُواْ ٱلزَّكَوٰةَۚ وَذَٰلِكَ دِينُ ٱلۡقَيِّمَةِ ۝٥

[6] Surely those People of the Book who are unbelievers, as well as the idol-worshippers will remain forever in the Hellfire. They are the worst of creation.

إِنَّ ٱلَّذِينَ كَفَرُواْ مِنۡ أَهۡلِ ٱلۡكِتَٰبِ وَٱلۡمُشۡرِكِينَ فِي نَارِ جَهَنَّمَ خَٰلِدِينَ فِيهَآۚ أُوْلَٰٓئِكَ هُمۡ شَرُّ ٱلۡبَرِيَّةِ ۝٦

---

109. Arabic – *ṣalāt wa zakāt* (also pronounced *ṣalāh wa zakāh*). These are two of the five pillars of Islam. To establish prayers does not mean just to pray by oneself, but to make sure that regular prayers are held by a community; for instance by building a mosque and calling people to prayer at the appointed times with the *adhān. Zakāt* does not mean that each person should simply give money to the needy as they like, but that the community leaders will collect a minimum amount of wealth from each person who can afford it, and then give it out to those who need it. (Giving to people on other occasions is also important, of course; this is called *ṣadaqah*.)

110. In Arabic, *dīn al-qayyimah,* the religion of the Prophet Ibrāhīm عليه السلام, the upright, and his inheritors.

[7] And surely those who have faith and do what is good are the best of creation.

إِنَّ ٱلَّذِينَ ءَامَنُوا۟ وَعَمِلُوا۟ ٱلصَّـٰلِحَـٰتِ
أُو۟لَـٰٓئِكَ هُمْ خَيْرُ ٱلْبَرِيَّةِ ۝٧

[8] Their reward is with their Lord: Gardens of Eden in which rivers flow, where they will live forever. Allah is pleased with them, and they are pleased with Him. That is for those who fear their Lord.

جَزَآؤُهُمْ عِندَ رَبِّهِمْ جَنَّـٰتُ عَدْنٍ
تَجْرِى مِن تَحْتِهَا ٱلْأَنْهَـٰرُ خَـٰلِدِينَ
فِيهَآ أَبَدًا ۖ رَّضِىَ ٱللَّهُ عَنْهُمْ وَرَضُوا۟ عَنْهُ ۚ
ذَٰلِكَ لِمَنْ خَشِىَ رَبَّهُۥ ۝٨

99

az-Zalzalah [The Earthquake]

MADĪNAN PERIOD

This *sūrah* is named after the great earthquakes of the Day of Resurrection, which will shake the earth repeatedly. All the souls who ever lived will be brought back to life again, and the earth will open to reveal all archeological artifacts and evidence of man's life on earth. People will at first be in shock, confused to find themselves awakened, and will wonder 'What is happening? What is wrong with the earth? What am I doing here?'; but the believers will soon realize that they have been called to their final Judgement.

It is interesting to learn here that the earth itself will come forth as a witness to testify about the evil that people did upon her soil, sins against God and each other. In other *surāhs* we learn that people's own tongues, hands and feet, eyes and ears, and even their skins will speak out about the deeds they committed with them.

All of this seemed strange to people of earlier times. It becomes easier to imagine with every new 'miracle' of science and technology, since we know that RNA and DNA store detailed information for every individual; tiny computer chips perform amazingly complicated functions; radio, TV and satellite waves travel vast distances unseen, and so on. In Western countries people have often thought that science and religious beliefs cannot go together, but Muslims have always be-lieved differently. The Qur'ān is a 'scientifically sound' book, and the discoveries of science can often serve to strengthen the faith of believers.[111]

The *sūrah* ends by explaining that every tiniest action will be remembered, and will be rewarded or punished accordingly. However, Allah in His kindness will reward believers at least ten times for each single act of goodness they have done. The Prophet ﷺ explained in several *aḥādīth* that believers will be cleansed of their sins through the sickness, pain and hardship they suffer during their lifetimes, and Allah will overlook our minor sins on Judgement Day if we have kept ourselves away from major sins. According to the Prophet ﷺ, in a famous *ḥadīth qudsī,* 'Allah, Exalted and Glorious, says: My Mercy is greater than My anger'.[112]

111. See introductory notes for *Sūrah* 96.
112. *Ḥadīth* from the collection of Muslim.

az-Zalzalah [The Earthquake]	سُورَةُ الزَّلْزَلَةِ
In the name of Allah, the All-Merciful, the Most Kind	بِسْمِ ٱللَّهِ ٱلرَّحْمَٰنِ ٱلرَّحِيمِ
[1] When the earth is shaken with her (final), mighty earthquake,	إِذَا زُلْزِلَتِ ٱلْأَرْضُ زِلْزَالَهَا ١
[2] and the earth releases her burdens,	وَأَخْرَجَتِ ٱلْأَرْضُ أَثْقَالَهَا ٢
[3] and people cry out: 'What is wrong with her?'	وَقَالَ ٱلْإِنسَٰنُ مَا لَهَا ٣
[4] On that day she will tell her story,	يَوْمَئِذٍ تُحَدِّثُ أَخْبَارَهَا ٤
[5] because your Lord has inspired her.	بِأَنَّ رَبَّكَ أَوْحَىٰ لَهَا ٥
[6] On that day (all) mankind will come forward in scattered groups, to be shown their deeds,	يَوْمَئِذٍ يَصْدُرُ ٱلنَّاسُ أَشْتَاتًا لِّيُرَوْا۟ أَعْمَٰلَهُمْ ٦

[7] and whoever has done an atom's weight[113] of good will see it then,

فَمَن يَعۡمَلۡ مِثۡقَالَ ذَرَّةٍ خَيۡرٗا يَرَهُۥ ٧

[8] and whoever has done an atom's weight of bad will see it then.

وَمَن يَعۡمَلۡ مِثۡقَالَ ذَرَّةٖ شَرّٗا يَرَهُۥ ٨

---

113. 'An atom's weight' – *dharrah* in Arabic; the tiniest amount that a person can imagine.

100

al-'Ādiyāt [The Charging Horses]

MAKKAN PERIOD

The first verses of this *sūrah* describe horses in battle in a powerful and poetic style. Horses are noble and brave creatures who can be trained to patiently perform many useful tasks for humans, although they prefer to be free by nature. They can be persuaded to keep moving even under dangerous and difficult conditions: crossing rivers, climbing mountains, and carrying their masters loyally through flying arrows or gunfire.

They were highly treasured by the Arabs, who developed one of the best breeds in the world: the Arabian horse, valued for its intelligence, speed, and ability to travel long distances. So, many scholars believe that horses are mentioned at the beginning of this *sūrah* in order to compare their good qualities with those of cowardly men who prefer to stay home to look after their worldly interests rather than go and fight. Several *ḥadīth* relate stories of a few rich *Ṣaḥābah* who were distracted from joining in *jihād* with the Prophet ﷺ out of concern for their property and possessions.

Another possible explanation is that the *sūrah* refers to the night raids that were common between Arab tribesmen before Islam. Out of their love for riches, men would use their horses for surprise attacks against enemy tribes at night or at dawn. They would grab as much as they could from the tents before their victims were awake enough to defend themselves, and then gallop away.

Regardless of how much wealth we might accumulate, we cannot take any of it with us when we die, and it will not help us in the least when we have to stand before our Lord for our final Judgement.

al-ʿĀdiyāt

[The Charging Horses]

سُورَةُ العَادِيَاتِ

In the name of Allah, the All-Merciful, the Most Kind

بِسْمِ ٱللَّهِ ٱلرَّحْمَٰنِ ٱلرَّحِيمِ

[1] By the charging horses,

وَٱلْعَٰدِيَٰتِ ضَبْحًا ١

[2] striking sparks of fire (with their hooves),

فَٱلْمُورِيَٰتِ قَدْحًا ٢

[3] attacking at dawn,

فَٱلْمُغِيرَٰتِ صُبْحًا ٣

[4] raising a trail of dust,

فَأَثَرْنَ بِهِۦ نَقْعًا ٤

[5] rushing straight on (into the enemy)!

فَوَسَطْنَ بِهِۦ جَمْعًا ٥

[6] Surely man is ungrateful to his Lord,

إِنَّ ٱلْإِنسَٰنَ لِرَبِّهِۦ لَكَنُودٌ ٦

[7] and he himself is witness to that (by his words and deeds).

وَإِنَّهُۥ عَلَىٰ ذَٰلِكَ لَشَهِيدٌ ٧

[8] And he is truly passionate in his love for wealth.

وَإِنَّهُۥ لِحُبِّ ٱلْخَيْرِ لَشَدِيدٌ ٨

[9] Does he not know that when the graves are emptied out,

أَفَلَا يَعْلَمُ إِذَا بُعْثِرَ مَا فِى ٱلْقُبُورِ ٩

[10] and the secrets of people's hearts[114] are brought out into the open,

وَحُصِّلَ مَا فِى ٱلصُّدُورِ ١٠

[11] on that day, their Lord will know everything about them?

إِنَّ رَبَّهُم بِهِمْ يَوْمَئِذٍ لَّخَبِيرٌۢ ١١

114. Literally, 'breasts'.

101

al-Qāri'ah [The Terrible Disaster]

MAKKAN PERIOD

This early Makkan *sūrah* briefly describes the terror of the Day of Judgement. People will be scattered and confused, like moths flying from place to place without a clear direction; and the mountains, which we think of as being so stable, will be no more solid than loose bits of wool, or cotton balls. Then, some time later, everyone's deeds will be weighed on a special scale in Allah's 'court of justice'. Those whose good deeds are heavier than their bad deeds will be rewarded with Paradise, while those whose bad deeds weigh heavier on the scale will be punished in Hell. For more detailed descriptions of the Judgement, see *Sūrahs* 71, 81, 82 and 84.

al-Qāriʿah

سُورَةُ القَارِعَة

[The Terrible Disaster]

In the name of Allah, the All-Merciful, the Most Kind

بِسۡمِ ٱللَّهِ ٱلرَّحۡمَٰنِ ٱلرَّحِيمِ

[1] The terrible disaster!

ٱلۡقَارِعَةُ ١

[2] What is the terrible disaster?

مَا ٱلۡقَارِعَةُ ٢

[3] O, what will make you understand what the terrible disaster is?

وَمَآ أَدۡرَىٰكَ مَا ٱلۡقَارِعَةُ ٣

[4] The day that people will be like thickly-scattered moths,

يَوۡمَ يَكُونُ ٱلنَّاسُ كَٱلۡفَرَاشِ
ٱلۡمَبۡثُوثِ ٤

[5] and the mountains will be like loose bits of wool.

وَتَكُونُ ٱلۡجِبَالُ كَٱلۡعِهۡنِ
ٱلۡمَنفُوشِ ٥

[6] Then whoever's scales are heavy (with faith and good deeds)

فَأَمَّا مَن ثَقُلَتۡ مَوَٰزِينُهُۥ ٦

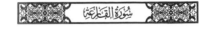

[7] will live a most pleasant life (in Paradise),	فَهُوَ فِي عِيشَةٍ رَّاضِيَةٍ ٧
[8] but whoever's scales are light –	وَأَمَّا مَنْ خَفَّتْ مَوَازِينُهُۥ ٨
[9] the bottomless pit will be his mother.[115]	فَأُمُّهُۥ هَاوِيَةٌ ٩
[10] And what will make you understand what it is?	وَمَآ أَدْرَىٰكَ مَا هِيَهْ ١٠
[11] A blazing fire!	نَارٌ حَامِيَةٌۢ ١١

115. The word 'mother' is used here to mean the place which will completely surround a person, like an unborn baby inside its mother.

102

at-Takāthur [Competition in Increasing Wealth]

MAKKAN PERIOD

This *sūrah* is a warning to people who spend much of their time trying to make more money, collect more material possessions, or have more children for the sake of being considered rich or important. This materialistic attitude is very common today, but is discouraged in Islam. The Prophet ﷺ lived a very simple life and encouraged his followers to do the same. We will all be questioned on the Last Day about everything that Allah has given us and what we have done with it: our health, wealth, talents and abilities, and the time and opportunities we were given to serve God and make a positive difference in other people's lives. The Prophet ﷺ said: 'On the Day of Resurrection, every servant of Allah will remain standing (before Him) until he is questioned about his life, how he spent it; his knowledge, what he did with it; his money, how he earned it and spent it, and his body, how he used it'.[116]

116. *Ḥadīth* from the collection of Tirmidhī and Dārimī.

at-Takāthur

[Competition for Worldly Success]

سُورَةُ التَّكَاثُرِ

In the name of Allah, the All-Merciful, the Most Kind

بِسۡمِ ٱللَّهِ ٱلرَّحۡمَٰنِ ٱلرَّحِيمِ

[1] Competition for worldly success distracts you

أَلۡهَىٰكُمُ ٱلتَّكَاثُرُ ١

[2] until you come to the graves.

حَتَّىٰ زُرۡتُمُ ٱلۡمَقَابِرَ ٢

[3] No, but you will soon find out!

كَلَّا سَوۡفَ تَعۡلَمُونَ ٣

[4] No! Surely you will come to know!

ثُمَّ كَلَّا سَوۡفَ تَعۡلَمُونَ ٤

[5] No, if you only knew (the truth) now with certainty

كَلَّا لَوۡ تَعۡلَمُونَ عِلۡمَ ٱلۡيَقِينِ ٥

[6] that you will surely see Hellfire (then you would change your ways).

لَتَرَوُنَّ ٱلۡجَحِيمَ ٦

[7] Yes indeed, you will certainly see it with clear vision.[117]

ثُمَّ لَتَرَوُنَّهَا عَيۡنَ ٱلۡيَقِينِ ٧

[8] Then, on that Day you will surely be questioned about the blessings and pleasures (you enjoyed).

ثُمَّ لَتُسۡـَٔلُنَّ يَوۡمَئِذٍ عَنِ ٱلنَّعِيمِ ٨

---

117. Literally 'with the eye of certainty'.

103

al-ʿAṣr [The Passing Time]

MAKKAN PERIOD

This is a very important *sūrah*; Imām Shāfiʿī said that if people thought carefully about it, it would be enough for their guidance. It is reported that when the *Ṣaḥābah* ﷺ met, they would recite it before they parted company.[118]

What makes this *sūrah* so special? It summarizes in a few words some main themes of the Qur'ān. Firstly, those who do not believe in God or do good deeds, or who spend their lives in lies and hypocrisy, will one day lose all that they have worked for. Their entire lives will have been wasted and it will be too late to do anything about it. In it we also see that those who do not struggle to establish truth in their lives and communities, or who give up their hopes or struggles too easily, will end up being losers. In every area of life it is necessary to have faith and always try to do one's best. We must encourage each other, whether our family, friends or other human beings, to strive for what is good and true, and to have patience even with things we dislike, if we wish to be successful.

Allah begins the *sūrah* by taking an oath in the name of 'passing time'. There is an interesting story which

118. *Ḥadīth* from the collection of Ṭabarānī.

makes clear the connection between time and the topic of this *sūrah.*[119] Before the age of refrigerators and freezers, storing ice for use in the summer was a difficult and delicate affair. A thousand years ago, residents of warm Muslim lands would transport huge blocks of snow and ice from neighbouring mountain peaks or bring them by camel and ship from special underground 'ice houses' where ice had been saved and insulated with salt and straw for use in the summer. Eventually this ice would find its place in the market, along with other goods for sale. One scholar reported that he understood the meaning of *'wa'l-ʿaṣr, inna'l-insāna lafī khusr'* when he heard an ice-seller in the market place calling out, 'Have mercy on a man whose wealth is melting away!' meaning, 'Please buy my ice before it melts, or I will lose all my investment and have no money with which to feed my family!' Of course, on a very hot day, even with the best of insulation the ice would melt with every passing second. The scholar thought about this. Our lives are like the blocks of ice: they are passing away with each second, never to return. Just as the ice-seller is a loser if he does not sell his merchandise before it melts, so are we losers if we do not make the most of our time by filling it with good deeds which will 'pay off' in the Life to Come.

---

119. Reported as a story from Imām Rāzī, by Mawdūdī (1988) in *The Meaning of the Qur'ān,* Vol. XVI, Lahore: Islamic Publications.

al-ʿAṣr

[The Passing Time]

سُورَةُ العَصۡرِ

In the name of Allah, the All-Merciful, the Most Kind

بِسۡمِ ٱللَّهِ ٱلرَّحۡمَٰنِ ٱلرَّحِيمِ

[1] By the passing time:

وَٱلۡعَصۡرِ ١

[2] people are definitely losers –

إِنَّ ٱلۡإِنسَٰنَ لَفِي خُسۡرٍ ٢

[3] except those who have faith and do good deeds, and encourage one another to the truth, and encourage one another to patiently endure.[120]

إِلَّا ٱلَّذِينَ ءَامَنُواْ وَعَمِلُواْ
ٱلصَّٰلِحَٰتِ وَتَوَاصَوۡاْ بِٱلۡحَقِّ
وَتَوَاصَوۡاْ بِٱلصَّبۡرِ ٣

---

120. The Arabic word *ṣabr* means endurance, or firm patience; carrying on under difficulties.

104

al-Humazah [The Slanderer]

MAKKAN PERIOD

In this *sūrah* Allah warns us against some bad qualities of character that are associated with a lack of *taqwā*. Backbiting is to say something about a person behind his back which he would not like to hear, even if it is true. Slander is to spread lies about a person and insult him, with the intention of making him look bad in the eyes of others (to say bad things about people to their face or call them names is also not allowed). Muslims should not gossip or speak badly about others in any way. The Prophet ﷺ taught, 'Whoever believes in Allah and the Last Day should say what is good, or be silent'.[121]

Greed is also condemned in this *sūrah*. Some people become so occupied with money that they forget they will die one day, and that none of their wealth will accompany them to the grave. People who live selfishly and waste their time in gossip may feel darkness in their souls during their earthly lives, and on the Last Day they will end up in Hellfire.

121. *Ḥadīth* from the collections of Bukhārī and Muslim.

al-Humazah

سُورَةُ الهُمَزَةِ

[The Slanderer]

In the name of Allah, the All-Merciful, the Most Kind

بِسْمِ ٱللَّهِ ٱلرَّحْمَٰنِ ٱلرَّحِيمِ

[1] Cursed is every back-biting slanderer (who finds fault with others)!

وَيْلٌ لِّكُلِّ هُمَزَةٍ لُّمَزَةٍ ﴿١﴾

[2] – who has hoarded his wealth and keeps counting it,

ٱلَّذِى جَمَعَ مَالًا وَعَدَّدَهُۥ ﴿٢﴾

[3] thinking that his wealth will make him live forever!

يَحْسَبُ أَنَّ مَالَهُۥٓ أَخْلَدَهُۥ ﴿٣﴾

[4] No, but he will surely be thrown to the Crushing One!

كَلَّا ۖ لَيُنۢبَذَنَّ فِى ٱلْحُطَمَةِ ﴿٤﴾

[5] And what can teach you what the Crushing One is?

وَمَآ أَدْرَىٰكَ مَا ٱلْحُطَمَةُ ﴿٥﴾

[6] It is the fire of Allah, kindled,

نَارُ ٱللَّهِ ٱلْمُوقَدَةُ ﴿٦﴾

[7] which reaches right into the hearts.	ٱلَّتِى تَطَّلِعُ عَلَى ٱلْأَفْـِٔدَةِ ﴿٧﴾
[8] Surely it closes in on them (from every side)	إِنَّهَا عَلَيْهِم مُّؤْصَدَةٌ ﴿٨﴾
[9] in towering columns.	فِى عَمَدٍ مُّمَدَّدَةٍ ﴿٩﴾

105

al-Fīl [The Elephant]

MAKKAN PERIOD

The Arabs before Islam used a lunar calendar to count the months and days, but they did not number their years; instead, they gave them names based on some special event that occurred during that year. The year of the Prophet Muḥammad's ﷺ birth was known as the 'Year of the Elephant' because of the story that follows.

An Abyssinian Christian general named Abraha rulled over Yemen at the time. He was irritated that so many pilgrims travelled to Makkah every year, taking their business and trade there. He decided to compete with the Makkans by building a big church in Ṣanʿā, hoping that people would come to visit it instead, so that Yemen would increase in wealth and importance. However, after he had invested a lot of time, money and effort in making a huge cathedral, the annual pilgrimage to Makkah continued as usual. Abraha then decided to destroy the Kaʿbah. He marched on Makkah with a large army and several elephants, which had never been seen in Makkah before.

The army was too great for the inhabitants of Makkah to resist. The only thing they could do was to try to save themselves by hiding in the mountains and caves around the city, leaving the Kaʿbah unprotected. The leader of the Quraysh at that time was 'Abd al-Muṭṭalib, the Prophet's ﷺ own grandfather. When the army advanced near Makkah they captured many animals belonging to the Quraysh, including 200 of 'Abd al-Muṭṭalib's camels. 'Abd al-Muṭṭalib then went to meet Abraha, to ask that his camels be returned to him. Abraha was surprised that he came to ask for his camels but said nothing about the great Ka'bah, but 'Abd al-Muṭṭalib answered: 'I am the owner of my camels and I ask you to return them. The House has its own owner, and He will defend it.' The rest of the Quraysh joined with 'Abd al-Muṭṭalib in praying to Allah, Lord of the Ka'bah, to save His House.

The first miracle that happened was that the chief elephant refused to walk in the direction of the Ka'bah. Then Allah destroyed the army by means of a flock of birds, which attacked the men with stones of clay which made them bleed heavily. Their wounds became infected with pus, and they soon died. The Ka'bah and Makkah were left unharmed.

Why did Allah remind the Quraysh of this story? The coming of the army with the elephants was a recent event in history for the Makkans; many men alive at the time of this Revelation still remembered the Year of the Elephant. They had run into the hills to escape, had gazed in wonder at the elephants, and had seen the dead bodies of the soldiers of Abraha lying in the outskirts of Makkah; possibly they had helped to quickly dig mass graves for them. The Makkans had prayed to Allah for His protection at the time of the invasion, and some had even returned to the faith of their forefather

Ibrāhīm ﷺ and worshipped One God alone for a number of years afterwards. Why, then, should they reject the miracle and message of the Qur'ān now – only 40 years later? How dared they oppose His Messenger ﷺ and risk arousing the anger of the Lord of the Worlds, Who had so easily destroyed Abraha and his army?

al-Fīl

[The Elephant]

سُورَةُ الفِيلِ

In the name of Allah, the All-Merciful, the Most Kind

بِسۡمِ ٱللَّهِ ٱلرَّحۡمَٰنِ ٱلرَّحِيمِ

[1] Have you not seen how your Lord dealt with the People of the Elephant?

أَلَمۡ تَرَ كَيۡفَ فَعَلَ رَبُّكَ بِأَصۡحَٰبِ
ٱلۡفِيلِ ١

[2] Did He not bring all their plans to nothing –

أَلَمۡ يَجۡعَلۡ كَيۡدَهُمۡ فِى تَضۡلِيلٖ ٢

[3] and send against them flocks of birds

وَأَرۡسَلَ عَلَيۡهِمۡ طَيۡرًا أَبَابِيلَ ٣

[4] which hurled against them stones of baked clay,

تَرۡمِيهِم بِحِجَارَةٖ مِّن سِجِّيلٖ ٤

[5] and made them become like dried grass, eaten up?

فَجَعَلَهُمۡ كَعَصۡفٖ مَّأۡكُولِۭ ٥

106

al-Quraysh [The Tribe of Quraysh]

MAKKAN PERIOD

The Prophet Muḥammad ﷺ was a member of the Quraysh, the most powerful and important tribe in Makkah. They were proud of their position and resisted the message of Islam for a long time. Now, to understand this *sūrah* one must know that Makkah is in the midst of a very hot desert and almost nothing can grow there. The Quraysh and the other residents of Makkah survived mainly through trading with their neighbours. In the winter they sent trade caravans southeast to Yemen, where they bought spices and other goods that had come from India and islands to the east. In the summer they sold these spices, silks and other products to the people in the northern lands of the Shām (Syria, Palestine, Jordan and Lebanon), from whom they bought various food products. While travelling they met many different people and became rich in their knowledge of human customs and cultures. Their other main source of income, as well as social and political benefits, was the yearly pilgrimage to the Ka'bah. This tradition dated back to the time of the Prophet Ibrāhīm عليه السلام, and people came from far and wide to complete it. This put the Quraysh in the position of hosts, and developed their sense of tolerance and hospitality. In return for this hospitality, they were respected and protected wherever they went. Although other caravans in Arabia feared attacks from highway robbers, the Qurayshi merchants travelled untouched.

The Quraysh were accustomed to their comfortable position, seldom needing to worry about food or safety. In this *sūrah* they were reminded to worship the true Lord of the Ka'bah, rather than the idols which had been put up around it, and to be thankful to the true Provider of all their needs.

al-Quraysh

[The Tribe of Quraysh]

سُورَةُ قُرَيۡشٍ

In the name of Allah, the All-Merciful, the Most Kind

بِسۡمِ ٱللَّهِ ٱلرَّحۡمَٰنِ ٱلرَّحِيمِ

[1] For the benefit[122] of the Quraysh;

لِإِيلَٰفِ قُرَيۡشٍ ١

[2] for their benefit the caravans go out in the winter and summer.

إِۦلَٰفِهِمۡ رِحۡلَةَ ٱلشِّتَآءِ وَٱلصَّيۡفِ ٢

[3] So they should worship the Lord of this House[123]

فَلۡيَعۡبُدُواْ رَبَّ هَٰذَا ٱلۡبَيۡتِ ٣

[4] Who has fed them, protecting them from hunger, and has made them safe from fear.

ٱلَّذِيٓ أَطۡعَمَهُم مِّن جُوعٖ وَءَامَنَهُم
مِّنۡ خَوۡفِۭ ٤

---

122. The word *īlāf* has many meanings; alternative translations include 'for the safety and security of the Quraysh' or 'to make the Quraysh tame, refined and civilized'.

123. The Ka'bah.

107

al-Mā'ūn [Simple Acts of Kindness]

MAKKAN PERIOD

In this *sūrah* Allah condemns people who pay close attention to ritual acts of worship such as *ṣalāh,* while ignoring the importance of helping others. It warns against being forgetful of one's prayers by not praying regularly or on time, or only praying at the last minute as a matter of habit. It also warns against hypocrisy, as shown by the person who offers extra prayers so that others can say that he is religious, rather than solely for the purpose of humbling himself before his Creator, in praise and gratitude.

al-Mā'ūn

سُورَةُ المَاعُون

[Simple Acts of Kindness]

In the name of Allah, the All-Merciful, the Most Kind

بِسۡمِ ٱللَّهِ ٱلرَّحۡمَٰنِ ٱلرَّحِيمِ

[1] Have you seen the one who denies religion?[124]

أَرَءَيۡتَ ٱلَّذِي يُكَذِّبُ بِٱلدِّينِ ١

[2] – the one who pushes orphans aside,

فَذَٰلِكَ ٱلَّذِي يَدُعُّ ٱلۡيَتِيمَ ٢

[3] and does not encourage (himself or others to) feed the poor?

وَلَا يَحُضُّ عَلَىٰ طَعَامِ ٱلۡمِسۡكِينِ ٣

[4] Oh, wretched are the worshippers

فَوَيۡلٞ لِّلۡمُصَلِّينَ ٤

[5] who are forgetful of their prayers –

ٱلَّذِينَ هُمۡ عَن صَلَاتِهِمۡ سَاهُونَ ٥

---

124. Or 'who denies the Judgement (Day)'.

[6] those who show off (in prayer and other good deeds)

ٱلَّذِينَ هُمْ يُرَآءُونَ ۝٦

[7] but refuse simple acts of kindness![125]

وَيَمْنَعُونَ ٱلْمَاعُونَ ۝٧

125. 'Simple acts of kindness' mean things such as what neighbours commonly ask of each other from day to day: to borrow a cooking pot, a hammer, sugar or coffee, or to water the plants when they are away on a trip, etc. People who refuse to do even these simple things for others are really hard-hearted and stingy.

108

al-Kawthar [The Abundance]

MAKKAN PERIOD

Some leaders of the Quraysh made fun of the Prophet Muḥammad ﷺ when his young son Qāsim died, saying that he no longer had any sons to carry on his name and that he would be forgotten after his death. Allah promised in this *sūrah* that instead it would be those people who insulted the Prophet ﷺ who would leave behind no one to remember them. 1400 years later, millions of Muslims worldwide ask Allah to shower His blessings on the Prophet Muḥammad ﷺ and his family and Companions ‎رضي الله عنهم‎ in every ritual prayer, as well as on many other occasions.

al-Kawthar

سُورَةُ الكَوْثَرِ

[The Abundance]

In the name of Allah, the All-Merciful, the Most Kind

بِسْمِ ٱللَّهِ ٱلرَّحْمَٰنِ ٱلرَّحِيمِ

[1] Surely We have given you (the Fountain of) Abundance[126]

إِنَّآ أَعْطَيْنَٰكَ ٱلْكَوْثَرَ ١

[2] so pray to your Lord, and make a sacrifice.

فَصَلِّ لِرَبِّكَ وَٱنْحَرْ ٢

[3] Surely it is he who insults you (Muḥammad, and not you) who will leave behind no one to remember him.

إِنَّ شَانِئَكَ هُوَ ٱلْأَبْتَرُ ٣

---

126. *Al-Kawthar* is the name of a fountain in Paradise; it means 'abundance' or plenty; more good than a person needs. Ibn 'Abbās ﵄ said about it: 'That is the good which Allah has given to His Messenger', and Sa'īd ibn Jubayr explained: 'The river (containing the Fountain or Pool of al-Kawthar) in Paradise is part of the good which Allah has given to His Messenger'. (*Ḥadīth* from the collection of Bukhārī.)

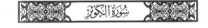

109

al-Kāfirūn [The Unbelievers]

MAKKAN PERIOD

The Makkans who resisted the Prophet's ﷺ message used to try to make compromises or 'deals' with him now and then to change Islam to something that they thought would be easier to practise. On one occasion some people said that they would worship only Allah for one year if the Prophet ﷺ would worship their idols the next year, and they could continue to take turns each year. So Allah revealed this *sūrah* to make it clear to the Quraysh that this was impossible, and also to show us how we should speak to unbelievers. If a person does not accept Islam after it has been explained to him, we should not argue but simply say, 'You have your way, I have mine.'

The Prophet ﷺ used to recite this *sūrah* along with *Sūrat al-Ikhlāṣ* in the *sunnah* prayer of *Ṣalāt al-Fajr*; he also recommended that Muslims recite it before going to sleep at night, as a protection against unbelief.[127]

127. *Ḥadīth* from the collections of Abū Dā'ūd, Tirmidhī and Nasā'ī.

al-Kāfirūn

سُورَةُ الكَافِرُونَ

[The Unbelievers]

In the name of Allah, the All-Merciful, the Most Kind

بِسْمِ ٱللَّهِ ٱلرَّحْمَٰنِ ٱلرَّحِيمِ

[1] Say: 'O unbelievers,

قُلْ يَٰٓأَيُّهَا ٱلْكَٰفِرُونَ ﴿١﴾

[2] I do not worship what you worship,

لَآ أَعْبُدُ مَا تَعْبُدُونَ ﴿٢﴾

[3] and you do not worship what I worship;

وَلَآ أَنتُمْ عَٰبِدُونَ مَآ أَعْبُدُ ﴿٣﴾

[4] and I will not worship what you worship,

وَلَآ أَنَا۠ عَابِدٌ مَّا عَبَدتُّمْ ﴿٤﴾

[5] and you do not worship what I worship.

وَلَآ أَنتُمْ عَٰبِدُونَ مَآ أَعْبُدُ ﴿٥﴾

[6] (So) for you is your way, and for me, mine.'

لَكُمْ دِينُكُمْ وَلِىَ دِينِ ﴿٦﴾

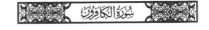

110

an-Naṣr [The Help]

MADĪNAN PERIOD

Sūrat an-Naṣr was the last complete *sūrah* of the Qur'ān to be revealed, on the occasion of the Farewell Pilgrimage three months before the Prophet's ﷺ death.[128] The *sūrah* itself was a sign from Allah that his mission had been completed and he could look forward to returning to his Lord in full favour. Only two years before, the holy city of Makkah had been peacefully reclaimed by an army of 10,000 Muslims, and had been cleansed of idolatry and all evil practices. Now as many as 100,000 believers accompanied the Prophet ﷺ on his Farewell Pilgrimage to the holy city! In that short time Islam had spread beyond Makkah and Madīnah to include all of Arabia. For the first time in recorded history, people had accepted – by the thousands – the prophethood of a man while he was still alive, and received him ﷺ as their leader and ruler. Tribe after tribe came to offer their allegiance to the beloved Muḥammad ﷺ, and merchants began to spread the message of Islam beyond the borders of Arabia. The mission of Muḥammad ﷺ had become clearly victorious through Allah's infinite grace.

128. A few *āyahs* of the Qur'ān were revealed after it, but no complete *sūrahs*.

There are few men who enjoy total fulfillment of their life's dreams and ambitions before they die. Those who do are usually quite proud of themselves. In contrast, Allah taught the Prophet ﷺ the beautiful manners of asking forgiveness for whatever lapses he may have unintentionally committed, and offering constant praise and thanks to his Lord, without Whom no success is possible.[129] Although these instructions are addressed to the beloved Prophet ﷺ, they are also meant generally, for all believers. Whenever someone is successful in any worthy project or undertaking, no matter how much he has sacrificed and how much good he has done, he must never forget to remain humble before his Lord, Creator and Sustainer of the Universe.

129. It is reported that from the time *Sūrat an-Naṣr* was revealed until the Prophet's death, he used to be found repeating over and over, *"Subḥānaka Allāhumma wa bi-ḥamdik, Allāhumma 'ghfir lī"*, meaning, 'Glory be to You, O Allah, and praise; please forgive me, O Allah!', and other similar phrases, since he considered this *sūrah* to be an order for him to do so.

an-Naṣr

[The Help]

سُورَةُ النَّصْرِ

بِسْمِ ٱللَّهِ ٱلرَّحْمَٰنِ ٱلرَّحِيمِ

In the name of Allah, the All-Merciful, the Most Kind

إِذَا جَآءَ نَصْرُ ٱللَّهِ وَٱلْفَتْحُ ﴿١﴾

[1] When Allah's help comes, and victory,

وَرَأَيْتَ ٱلنَّاسَ يَدْخُلُونَ فِى دِينِ
ٱللَّهِ أَفْوَاجًا ﴿٢﴾

[2] and you see people coming into Allah's religion in masses,

فَسَبِّحْ بِحَمْدِ رَبِّكَ وَٱسْتَغْفِرْهُ ۚ إِنَّهُۥ
كَانَ تَوَّابًۢا ﴿٣﴾

[3] then (remember to) praise your Lord and ask Him for forgiveness. Surely He is always ready to forgive.

111

al-Masad [The Palm Leaf]

MAKKAN PERIOD

Abū Lahab and his wife did many terrible, almost unbelievable things to the Prophet ﷺ and his Companions ‎. Although he was the Prophet's ﷺ own uncle, he tried in every way to make his life miserable. He is the only person mentioned in the Qur'ān specifically by name for Allah's punishment. His wife used to get up early in the morning to collect thorns to put in front of the Prophet's ﷺ house. It is said that she owned a valuable necklace, which she wanted to sell so that she could use the money to harm the Prophet ﷺ in some way. Allah says here that rather than a necklace, she will have a rough rope around her neck in Hell. This *sūrah* is also known as *al-Lahab* (the Flame).

al-Masad

[The Palm Leaf]

سُورَةُ المَسَد

In the name of Allah, the All-Merciful, the Most Kind

بِسْمِ ٱللَّهِ ٱلرَّحْمَٰنِ ٱلرَّحِيمِ

[1] May the power[130] of Abū Lahab perish! He will perish.

تَبَّتْ يَدَآ أَبِي لَهَبٍ وَتَبَّ ﴿١﴾

[2] Neither his wealth nor what he has earned has helped him.[131]

مَآ أَغْنَىٰ عَنْهُ مَالُهُۥ وَمَا كَسَبَ ﴿٢﴾

[3] He will be pushed down into the flaming Fire,

سَيَصْلَىٰ نَارًا ذَاتَ لَهَبٍ ﴿٣﴾

[4] and (so will) his wife, the wood-carrier.

وَٱمْرَأَتُهُۥ حَمَّالَةَ ٱلْحَطَبِ ﴿٤﴾

[5] She will have a rope of rough palm leaves around her neck.

فِي جِيدِهَا حَبْلٌ مِّن مَّسَدٍ ﴿٥﴾

---

130. Literally, 'the hands '.

131. According to Ibn 'Abbās ﵁, 'what he has earned, or gained' means his children and grandchildren.

112

al-Ikhlāṣ [Purity, or Sincerity]

MAKKAN PERIOD

This is one of the most important *sūrahs* because it describes Allah's Oneness, or *tawḥīd*, the central Islamic belief about God. We know from several *aḥādīth* that it was revealed in response to questions the Makkans asked the Prophet ﷺ about the nature of Allah. The idolators asked: 'Tell us of your Lord's ancestry'; some Jews asked: '... Allah created the angels from light, Adam from clay, Iblīs (Satan) from the flame of fire, the sky from smoke, and the earth from the foam of water. Now tell us about your Lord (what he is made of).' A group of Christians came and asked: 'O Muḥammad, tell us what your Lord is like and of what substance He is made.'[132] In each case, the Prophet ﷺ answered with this *sūrah*.

What is the right way to understand the Oneness of God, Allah? It is not in the sense of numbers and counting, because the word *aḥad* is not the same as the Arabic word *wāḥid* which is used for the number one. Allah is One in the sense that He is Unique, and there is nothing like Him anywhere that He could be compared with. He is not one of a group of 'gods and goddesses' who fall in love, marry, plot against each other or

132. *Ḥadīth* from the collection of Bukhārī.

put silly curses on humans, as the ancient Greeks and many other people used to believe. He cannot be divided into parts, such as in the Christian concept of the Trinity in which, in one way or another, three gods or parts of God are believed to merge into one. He is not in need of anything; He does not have a father, and He does not need a wife for company or a son to help Him. He is not a father, although He provides everything for His creatures as a father does; and He does not have children, although those who follow His commandments are well-loved by Him, as a human father might love those of his children who are good and obedient. Allah is more merciful to His creatures than a mother is to her beloved child, and more pleased when a servant of His repents than a man is who loses his camel in the hot desert, and lies down, expecting to die, and then finds it again. He is the Eternal One Who never dies, the Guide and Protector whom everyone calls upon when they are in desperate need of help, Who does whatever He wills in His perfect wisdom.

The Prophet Muḥammad ﷺ said that *al-Ikhlāṣ* is equal to one-third of the Qur'ān, and that we should recite it often. A man came to the Prophet ﷺ and said, 'O Messenger of Allah, I love *Sūrat al-Ikhlāṣ*'. The Prophet ﷺ told him, 'Love of it will admit you to Paradise' [Tirmidhī].

al-Ikhlāṣ

سُورَةُ الإخلاص

[Purity, or Sincerity]

In the name of Allah, the All-Merciful, the Most Kind

بِسۡمِ ٱللَّهِ ٱلرَّحۡمَٰنِ ٱلرَّحِيمِ

[1] Say: 'Allah is One (God).

قُلۡ هُوَ ٱللَّهُ أَحَدٌ ١

[2] Allah is the Eternal One.

ٱللَّهُ ٱلصَّمَدُ ٢

[3] He does not give birth, He was not born,

لَمۡ يَلِدۡ وَلَمۡ يُولَدۡ ٣

[4] and there is nothing (at all) like Him.'

وَلَمۡ يَكُن لَّهُۥ كُفُوًا أَحَدُۢ ٤

113 & 114

al-Muʿawwidhatān

[The Two *Sūrahs* of Seeking Refuge in Allah]

MAKKAN PERIOD

The last two *sūrahs* of the Qur'ān, *al-Falaq* and *an-Nās*, were revealed together and are usually recited together, so their joint explanation is given here.

These *sūrahs* were revealed to the Prophet ﷺ at a time when his health and memory had been slightly affected by witchcraft or black magic as practised on him by a Jewish man in Madīnah named Labīd. This man had gotten hold of some of the Prophet's ﷺ hair and put a spell on it, which led to him feeling tired, weak, and sometimes confused about whether or not he had done something or gone somewhere. Then the Prophet ﷺ had a dream about the spell and how to overcome it, and when he awoke the Angel Jibrā'īl عليه السلام came bringing him these two *sūrahs* and confirmed that his dream was a true one. Before their revelation the Prophet ﷺ used to say various *duʿā's* against all kinds of illnesses, troubles and evils; after they were revealed he abandoned all other prayers and repeated these over and over, urging his followers to do the same.

'Seeking refuge' means to ask for protection and help from someone against something which you feel powerless to face or handle. The right attitude for be-lievers, when we face any difficulty, is to realize that we have no power by ourselves, but only what Allah may give us. Although everything that Allah has created is good in its own way and has its own special purpose, evil does appear from some of His creatures. The evil work of devils, *jinn* or magic, or the effects of the 'negative vibrations' of hatred and jealousy, and even negative thought patterns and emotions, are unpleasant to think of, but very real. Rather than look to anyone or anything else to help us, the best thing to do is to seek help from our Lord, the One Who created us in the first place and has complete power over us. Whenever we may be faced with a trying situation such as hunger, the death of a family member, losing our job, an unexplainable or serious illness, a fire or accident, being bitten by a snake or scorpion, or being attacked by criminals, we should recite *sūrahs al-Falaq* and *an-Nās,* repeatedly as necessary. These *sūrahs* should also be recited in the face of 'invisible' enemies: when a person feels that he is unable to concentrate in his prayer or has been unable to pray on time as usual, when feeling sad or depressed, angry or overcome by other strong emotions, when troubled by the hatred or jealousy of others, when he has been a victim of gossip or slander, and so forth.

These words of comfort, light and protection come as a beautiful conclusion to God's final Book of Revelation; a generous and merciful gift from the Lord of all the Worlds.

al-Falaq

[The Dawn]

سُورَةُ الفَلَقِ

In the name of Allah, the All-Merciful, the Most Kind

بِسْمِ ٱللَّهِ ٱلرَّحْمَٰنِ ٱلرَّحِيمِ

[1] Say: 'I seek protection with the Lord of the dawn

قُلْ أَعُوذُ بِرَبِّ ٱلْفَلَقِ ١

[2] from the evil of all that He created,

مِن شَرِّ مَا خَلَقَ ٢

[3] and from the evil of the darkness when it spreads (and intensifies),[133]

وَمِن شَرِّ غَاسِقٍ إِذَا وَقَبَ ٣

[4] and from the evil of those who practise witchcraft,[134]

وَمِن شَرِّ ٱلنَّفَّٰثَٰتِ فِى ٱلْعُقَدِ ٤

[5] and from the evil of an envious one when he envies.'

وَمِن شَرِّ حَاسِدٍ إِذَا حَسَدَ ٥

---

133. The forces of evil in the world are strongest at night and in the dark; many crimes and evil or sinful acts are committed at that time.

134. Literally, 'the women who blow on knots': in other words, witches.

an-Nās

[The People]

سُورَةُ النَّاسِ

In the name of Allah, the All-Merciful, the Most Kind

بِسْمِ ٱللَّهِ ٱلرَّحْمَٰنِ ٱلرَّحِيمِ

[1] Say: 'I seek protection with the Lord of all people,

قُلْ أَعُوذُ بِرَبِّ ٱلنَّاسِ ١

[2] the King of all people,

مَلِكِ ٱلنَّاسِ ٢

[3] the (true) God of all people,

إِلَٰهِ ٱلنَّاسِ ٣

[4] from the evil of the sneaking whisperer (Satan),

مِن شَرِّ ٱلْوَسْوَاسِ ٱلْخَنَّاسِ ٤

[5] who whispers (evil) into people's hearts,

ٱلَّذِى يُوَسْوِسُ فِى صُدُورِ ٱلنَّاسِ ٥

[6] whether from *jinn*s or humans.[135]

مِنَ ٱلْجِنَّةِ وَٱلنَّاسِ ٦

---

135. The evil whisperings of Satan (Shayṭan) can come from other people or from *jinn*.

Arabic Names and their Common English Equivalents

Arabic place names, names of the Prophets and angels have been used throughout this book; their commonly used English equivalents are given below for clarity.

Arabic	*English*
Allah	God
Jibrā'īl	Gabriel
Nūḥ	Noah
Ibrāhīm	Abraham
Isḥāq	Isaac
Ismā'īl	Ishmael
Mūsā	Moses
'Īsā	Jesus
Muḥammad	Mohammed
Makkah	Mecca
Madīnah	Medina
Qur'ān	Koran
'Īd	Eid

Glossary of Arabic Terms

Ādāb (singular *adab*) – manners or etiquette; the proper way of behaviour for a Muslim in all situations.

Adhān – the 'call to prayer', usually recited from the minaret of a mosque to let the believers know that the time for the *ṣalāh* has begun.

Astaghfirullāh – 'I seek Allah's forgiveness'; used in a variety of situations when a sin has been committed by oneself or others.

Āyah – literally 'a sign' (of Allah); a verse of the Qur'ān.

Dhikr – 'the remembrance' (of Allah), or keeping God in one's memory constantly; usually refers to saying key words and phrases repeatedly in a prayerful way, such as *Ṣubḥānallāh* (glory be to Allah), *astaghfirullāh* (I seek Allah's forgiveness), etc.

Du'ā' – 'supplicatory prayer'; a prayer made by an individual or group, usually to ask Allah for something. Unlike the *ṣalāh,* this kind of prayer is formed directly in the heart and can be made in any language at any time. The Prophet said, '*Du'ā'* is the heart of *'ibādah* (worship)', meaning that this open communication between a servant and his Lord is the most essential part of worship.

Ḥadīth (pl. *aḥādīth*) – a saying of the Prophet Muḥammad ﷺ. Certain Companions of the Prophet رضي الله عنهم memorized and passed on to others whatever they could of the Prophet's sayings and actions. These were later checked for accuracy according to very strict standards and then compiled in collections. Six of these collections are considered to be the most authentic and reliable (although there are several other outstanding ones); they are those of Bukhārī, Muslim, Tirmidhī, Abū Dā'ūd, Nasā'ī and Ibn Mājah.

Ḥadīth qudsī – (literally, 'Holy Tradition') is a special category of *ḥadīth* which contains saying of Allah, related by the Prophet Muḥammad ﷺ. It does not mean the actual Word of Allah, rather its meaning. This makes it distinct from the Qur'ān, which is the actual Word of Allah revealed to the Prophet ﷺ through the archangel Jibrā'īl عليه السلام.

Ḥalāl – permitted in Islamic law. In principle, everything is considered *ḥalāl* in Islam unless it has been specifically forbidden by Allah or the Prophet ﷺ. Allah has made the world clean and beautiful and most things are good and permissible.

Ḥarām – forbidden in Islamic law, 'off-limits'; something which is bad and for which a Muslim may be punished by Allah.

I'tikāf – to enter a mosque or a secluded area for a period of time to devote oneself entirely to worship. The Prophet ﷺ and many of his *Ṣaḥābah* ﵃ used to spend the last ten days of Ramaḍān in the mosque in *i'tikāf*.

Jihād – literally, 'to struggle'. In Islam it stands for all forms of striving, including armed struggle, strictly for the cause of Allah.

Jinn – an independent species of creation, created by Allah out of fire. These invisible beings inhabit their own world and they do not normally interfere in human life. As stated in *Sūrat al-Jinn* (72) some *Jinns* also believe in Islam.

Khuṭbah – the sermon or speech given by the Imām before the Friday congregational prayer (*Ṣalāt al-Jum'ah*).

Qiblah – the direction a Muslim faces during *ṣalāh*; the shortest distance to the Ka'bah in Makkah from wherever one is standing (which can be in any direction depending on where you live).

Rak'ah – a 'unit' or 'cycle' of *ṣalāh*; a group of positions which is repeated during the daily prayers, from raising the hands in the beginning to making the second prostration (or sitting) at the end.

Rizq – provision; what Allah has destined for a person and sends down, such as their income, food, and clothing.

Ṣadaqah – charity; to share what you have with others. Charity includes not only giving money or food, but also helping people in every way; even smiling and greeting others is considered a charity and will be rewarded.

Ṣaḥābah – a Companion of the Prophet Muḥammad ﷺ; technically, any Muslim who met the Prophet ﷺ during his lifetime. Muslims hold them in much esteem for their sacrifices, piety, excellent conduct and great love of the Prophet Muḥammad ﷺ. The Qur'ān says that 'Allah is well pleased with them' (*al-Fatḥ* 48:18).

Sajdah – to prostrate oneself on the ground to Allah, touching seven parts of the body to the ground: the two feet, two knees, two hands, and the forehead to the nose.

Ṣalāh – the ritual prayer which must be offered at least five times a day by every adult Muslim. The *ṣalāh* has a number of conditions which must be fulfilled in order for it to be accepted: it must be done at certain times, in specific positions, with recitations which must be said in Arabic, and so forth. In this way it is different from the simple 'prayer from the heart' which is called *duʿā'* (see above).

Shahādah – 'the witnessing' (of the truth); to become a Muslim by declaring one's belief in One God and His Final Messenger, and accepting the other major points of Islamic belief.

Sharī'ah – the Islamic way of life (often used interchangeably to mean Islamic Law).

Sīrah – a biography; it means the study of the life of the Prophet Muḥammad ﷺ.

Sunnah – habits and customs; it means the Prophet's daily customs and way of life.

Sūrah – literally 'wall'; a 'chapter' of the Qur'ān. The Qur'ān is made up of 114 *sūrahs* of widely differing lengths. *Sūrahs* are not chapters in the English sense of the word, organized around a particular topic, but arrangements of verses in a particular order which are often recited in one reading.

Tafsīr – commentary on the Qur'ān, including explanation of the meanings of words and verses, descriptions of the occasion of revelation, comparison of other *āyahs* or *ḥadīths* on the same topic, etc. *Tafsīr* was one of the first and most important religious sciences developed by Muslims, in order to help people understand the Qur'ān better and to avoid misinterpretations.

Tajwīd – the art of Qur'ānic recitation, pronouncing every letter clearly and distinctly in a beautiful tone.

Ṭaqwā – piety, righteousness, godfearingness, God-consciousness.

Tawbah – to turn away from sin; repentance; to ask Allah sincerely for forgiveness for a particular sin (or sins) with the intention of avoiding it in the future.

Tawḥīd – the essence of Islam; meaning to affirm God's Oneness and Unity. It also represent a commitment to worship, serve, and obey Him, and dedicate one's life to Him alone.

Ummah – nation, people, followers of a Prophet; often used to mean 'the Muslims'.

Wuḍū' – ablution; the ritual cleaning of the body before beginning an act of worship (including making the proper intention, washing the hands, mouth, nose, face, arms to the elbows, head, ears, neck and feet to the ankles). *Wuḍū'* is required before offering *ṣalāh* or reciting the Qur'ān, and is recommended for many other occasions.

Zakāt (also read as *zakāh*) – literally, 'the purification' (of wealth); the purifying charity, one of the five 'pillars of Islam', is collected once a year, being obligatory for every Muslim who can afford it, and given to the poor and needy.

Guide for Further Reading

OTHER QUR'ĀN TRANSLATIONS

There are now many good translations available of the entire Qur'ān in English, both in print and online. The most widely used is the classic translation and commentary by Abdullah Yusuf Ali, *The Meaning of the Holy Qur'ān,* written in elegant, though rather dated, English. A revised, more readable version has been published by Amana Publications.

For young people and adults who prefer a more accessible translation in modern English, Zafar Ishaq Ansari has produced an abridged version of Mawlana Mawdudi's *Towards Understanding the Qur'ān,* available in paperback, hardcover and compact bilingual editions. The facing columns of Arabic and English text make this a good choice for those who like to have the English meaning immediately available when reciting in Arabic.

Two recommended English-only versions are Professor Abdel Haleem's *The Qur'an: a new translation,* whose pocket-sized modern English text is arranged in paragraph form, and Dr. Thomas Cleary's full-sized *The Qur'an: A New Translation,* which has been laid out in verse, and is more elegant and readable as a result. Both should be accessible to able readers from age 12+.

Abdel Haleem, M. A. S. (2004). *The Qur'an: A new translation*. Oxford: Oxford University Press.

Ali, Abdullah Yusuf (1991) *The Meaning of the Holy Qur'an*. New edition with revised translation and commentary. Beltsville, Maryland (USA): Amana Publications. www.amana-publications.com

Cleary, Thomas (2004) *The Qur'an*: a *New Translation*. Burr Ridge, Illinois (USA): Starlatch Press.

Mawdūdī, Sayyid Abul 'Ala' (2006) *Towards Understanding the Qur'ān*: *abridged version of Tafhim al-Qur'ān*. Translated and Edited by Zafar Ishaq Ansari. Markfield: The Islamic Foundation.

Other English translations as well as the full Qur'anic text in Arabic can be found online at the following websites, among others. As websites change frequently, you may wish to conduct your own search.

www.quranonline.net
www.quranexplorer.com
http://www.usc.edu/schools/college/crcc/engagement/resources/texts/muslim/quran/
http://www.quranflash.com/en/quranflash.html
http://al-quran.info

QUR'ANIC STUDIES

Learning to read Arabic and recite the Qur'an with proper pronunciation is one of the fundamentals of a good Islamic education. While the best results can only be obtained through the personal guidance of a qualified teacher, books, computer software and internet programmes can go a long way towards meeting the need for instruction. AbdulWahid Hamid's complete courses are ideal for beginners: *Easy Steps in Qur'an Reading* teaches the (Urdu-style) Arabic script common to the Indo-Pakistani subcontinent, while *Graded Steps in Qur'an Reading* teaches the 'Uthmani script widely used throughout the rest of the Muslim world. Both sets include pupil and teacher/self-study editions, accompanying CD or audiotapes, and handwriting workbooks; posters and Arabic alphabet flash cards are also available. Use *Easy Steps* for ages 6+ and *Graded Steps* for 8+ through adult, and supplement with Dr. Alawiye's excellent flash cards for additional reading practice.

Alawiye, Imran (2005) *Gateway to Arabic Flash Cards, Set One: Letter Recognition and Reading Skills*. Gateway to Arabic series. Greenford (UK): Anglo Arabic Graphics. www.greatwaytoarabic.com.

Hamid, Abdulwahid (2003) *Easy Steps in Qur'an Reading*. London: MELS (Muslim Education and Literary Services). www.melspublications.com

For introductory books on how best to study the Qur'ān and benefit from its meaning and message, start with Khalid

Shaykh's textbook, *A Study of the Qur'an and its Teachings*, recommended for ages 10-14. Older teens and adults will appreciate Khurram Murad's *Way to the Qur'an* for its clear, concise and inspirational style, and Furber's translation of Imam al-Nawawī's *Etiquettes with the Qur'an* for its comprehensive treatment of *ahadith* on the subject.

Furber, Musa (2003) *Etiquettes with the Qur'an*. Translation of Imam al-Nawawi's *al-Tibyān fī Ādāb Ḥamalat al-Qur'ān*. Chicago: Starlatch Press.

Murad, Khurram (1985) *Way to the Qur'ān*. Leicester: Islamic Foundation.

Shaykh, Khalid Mahmood (1999) *A Study of the Qur'an and Its Teachings*. Chicago: IQRA' Educational Foundation.

HADITH, MORALS AND MANNERS

After the Qur'ān, the Aḥādīth and personal example of the beloved Prophet Muḥammad ﷺ are next in importance as a wellspring of guidance and foundation of Islamic life and culture. Reading a few Aḥādīth together as a family daily, perhaps after one of the prescribed prayers, can form the beginning of a lifelong habit. Chachi and D'Oyen's bilingual selection, *In the Prophet's Garden*, provides a good starting point for Ḥadīth study, with its thematically-arranged collection of 200 authentic sayings of the Prophet*, presented in simple, modern English for ages 8+. For older children and adults, Ezzeddin and Davies's able translations of Imām al-Nawawī's classics, *Forty Hadith* and *Forty Hadith Qudsi*, introduce some of the most significant Prophetic Traditions that every Muslim should be familiar with.

A new abridgement of a classical, thematic collection suitable for ages 14+, is Gai Eaton's dual-language selection from the *Mishkāt al-Maṣābīḥ*, entitled *The Book of Hadith.* For those who are ready for a more comprehensive treatment of the subject, Imam al-Nawawi's *Riyāḍ al-Ṣāliḥīn* (Gardens of the Righteous), comprising over 1900 *Aḥādīth*, is perhaps the most popular *Ḥadīth* collection of all time. There are a number of English translations, of varying quality.

Shaykh Hamza Yusuf's translation of 130 Aḥādīth, entitled *The Content of Character: Ethical Sayings of the Prophet Muhammad*, is a beautifully produced, compact dual-language edition suitable for ages 12+. The choice of brief sayings of the Prophet ﷺ make the collection particularly suitable for memorisation. For a more structured approach to the study of Islamic manners and good character, Aisha Lemu's *Islamic Tahdhib and Akhlaq: Theory and Practice* is a well-written introductory textbook for ages 9-13. Besides providing a thorough discussion of forty virtues and vices, it also contains brief biographies of several Prophets, the Rightly-Guided Caliphs, and the founders of the main schools of Islamic jurisprudence. Older readers will appreciate Shaykh Abu Ghudda's concise *Islamic Manners*, which provides guidance on Islamic etiquettes for most everyday situations.

Abu Ghudda, Shaykh Abdul Fattah (2001) *Islamic Manners*. Swansea, UK : Awakening Publications.

Chachi, A. K. and D'Oyen, F. M. (2009) *In the Prophet's Garden: A selection of ahadith for the young*. Markfield: The Islamic Foundation.

Eaton, Charles Le Gai (2008) *The Book of Hadith: Sayings of the Prophet Muhammad, from the* Mishkat al-Masabih. Selected by Charles Le Gai Eaton. Bristol: The Book Foundation.

Ibrahim, Ezzeddin and Johnson-Davies, Denys (1997) *An-Nawawi's Forty Hadith*. Cambridge: Islamic Texts Society.

Ibrahim, Ezzeddin and Johnson-Davies, Denys (1997) *Forty Hadith Qudsi*. Cambridge: Islamic Texts Society.

Lemu, B. Aisha (2001) *Islamic Tahdhib and Akhlaq: Theory and Practice*. Chicago: IQRA' Educational Foundation.

Yusuf, Hamza (2005) *The Content of Character: Ethical Sayings of the Prophet Muhammad*. Collected by Shaykh Al Amin Ali Mazrui. Sandala. info@sandala.net.

LIFE OF THE PROPHET MUHAMMAD ﷺ

Muslims should learn and benefit from the life story of the beloved Messenger of Allah ﷺ at every age. We suggest that parents and educators read and discuss a biography of the Prophet Muhammad ﷺ with children and teens every two years, alternating with stories of the earlier Prophets ﷺ. Leila Azzam's *The Life of the Prophet Muhammad* is a lovely presentation of the *Sīrah* with accurate and tasteful illustrations, recommended for ages 9+ (or 7+ if you read it aloud). Sayyed Abul Hasan Ali Nadwi's *Muhammad, the Last Prophet: a Model for All Time* is another highly recommended title for this age group. To help children gain a deeper appreciation for the Prophet's ﷺ lofty character, customs and habits, Abidullah Ghazi's *The Life of Perfection: Shamā'il of Rasūlullāh* would be a sound choice.

Tahia Al-Ismail's *The Life of Muḥammad* introduces brief analyses of social, historical and political issues yet remains fast-paced and easy to read, making it suitable for young adults 14+ and a good choice for adults who prefer everyday language. For those who enjoy a more challenging read, Martin Lings' elegant and inspiring *Muhammad: his life based on the earliest sources* is masterfully written, and is also available in an abridged version as an audiobook on CD or audiocassette. Alternatively, Adil Salahi's *Muḥammad: Man and Prophet* provides a sound, vivid and readable narrative and is recommended for ages 16+.

Al-Ismail, Tahia (1988) *The Life of Muḥammad*. London: Ta-Ha Publishers, Ltd.

Azzam, Leila and Gouvernour, Aisha (1985) *The Life of the Prophet Muhammad*. Cambridge (UK): The Islamic Texts Society.

Ghazi, Abidullah (1996) *The Life of Perfection: Shamā'il of Rasūlullāh*. Chicago: IQRA' Educational Foundation.

Lings, Martin (1991) *Muhammad: his life based on the earliest sources.* Cambridge (UK): Islamic Texts Society.

Lings, Martin (2003) *Muhammad: his life based on the earliest sources.* Narrated by Sean Barrett. Audiobook, available as set of CDs or audiocassettes. Birmingham (UK): MeemAudio. www.meem.info

Nadwi, Sayyed Abul Hasan Ali (1993) *Muhammad, the Last Prophet: a Model for All Time*. Leicester: UK Islamic Academy.

Salahi, Adil (2002) *Muḥammad: Man and Prophet*. Markfield: The Islamic Foundation.

LIVES OF THE PROPHETS

There are many books for younger children which recount the illuminating stories of the prophets ﷺ mentioned in the Qur'ān, but few that are suitable for older children or young adults. For children 7+, the scholar Sayyed Abul Hasan Ali Nadwi's *Stories of the Prophets* is well-written, and most children should find it interesting despite its lack of illustrations. Young people 12+ will appreciate Elma Harder's *Lives of the Prophets*, an engaging account of eleven prophets based solely on Qur'ānic narratives. It lacks some of the clarification offered by the *Ḥadīth* literature, most notably on the story of the Prophets Ibrāhīm عليه السلام, Ismā'īl عليه السلام and Hajar, but the author is otherwise to be commended for carefully avoiding non-authoritative additions to Qur'ānic accounts. Charming, simple illustrations enhance the text.

For older readers and adults who wish to fully examine the lives of all the prophets mentioned in the Qur'ān, Suzanne Hanif's meticulously researched, two-volume *A History of the Prophets of Islam* is a wonderful achievement, and the only reference most people are likely to need on the subject.

Hanif, Suzanne (2002) *A History of the Prophets of Islam: derived from the Qu'rān, Aḥādīth and Commentaries.* Volumes I and II. Chicago: Library of Islam; Kazi Publications, Inc.

Harder, Elma Ruth (2006) *Lives of the Prophets.* Karachi: Oxford University Press. Also available from Al-Qalam Publishers, Canada. *www.al-qalam.org*.

Nadwi, Sayyed Abul Hasan Ali (2007) *Stories of the Prophets.* Leicester: UK Islamic Academy.

BIOGRAPHIES OF THE NOBLE COMPANIONS

The Prophet's noble family and Companions made extraordinary sacrifices to establish and spread the message of Islam, and every Muslim should be familiar with at least forty of them. Noura Durkee's series of *Stories of the Ṣaḥāba* presents imaginative and inspiring accounts written in a lively style, suitable for 9+. Able readers from 12+ who can manage challenging vocabulary will appreciate AbdulWahid Hamid's two-volume set on *Companions of the Prophet,* which recounts the lives of 60 prominent male and female Ṣaḥāba in a captivating and inspirational manner. The latter is also available abridged, as an audiobook on CD. Older readers and adults will appreciate Imām al-Ghazālī's insightful discussion of *The Duties of Brotherhood in Islam*, ably translated by Mukhtar

Holland, which includes remarkable examples from the lives of the Companions, their successors and the early Muslims.

Durkee, Noura (1999-2005) *Stories of the Sahaba Series*, Volumes 1-5. Chicago: IQRA' Educational Foundation. Vol. 1 (2005): *Those Promised Paradise*. Vol. 2 (1999): *The First Ones*. Vol. 3: (1999) *Loyal Ansar*. Vol. 4: (2000) *Hearts Have Changed*. Vol. 5: (2000) *Torchbearers of Islam*.

Hamid, AbdulWahid (1995) *Companions of the Prophet* (Volumes 1 and 2, New Revised Edition). Leicester: Muslim Education and Literary Services. *www.melspublications.com*

Hamid, AbdulWahid. *Companions of the Prophet*. Narrated by Dawud Wharnsby Ali. 5-CD set. Bridgeview, Illinois (USA): Sound Vision.

Holland, Mukhtar (1992) *The Duties of Brotherhood in Islam. Translated from the Iḥyā' of Imām al-Ghazālī*. Markfield: The Islamic Foundation.

ISLAMIC STUDIES (GENERAL)

Many decent textbooks in English on Islamic Studies are now available, for a variety of needs and tastes. For upper primary/ elementary and middle school pupils, we recommend Hajiyah Aisha Lemu's *Islamic Aqidah and Fiqh* for its readable style, born of the author's long experience and understanding of children. IQRA's revised edition presents a very simple 'multi-*madhhab*' approach to *fiqh*, suitable for most classroom situations in the USA and Europe. Buy together with her *Islamic Tahdhib and Akhlaq: Theory and Practice* (reviewed under Hadith, Morals and Manners, above) for a complete introductory course on Islamic Studies.

Older middle school, secondary pupils and adults who wish to review basic teachings will find Ghulam Sarwar's *Islam: Beliefs and Teachings,* now in its 8th edition, to be a clear, concise and straightforward textbook. For young adults and new Muslims, or able readers 14+ with a more philosophical bent, AbdulWahid Hamid's *Islam, the Natural Way,* is an excellent choice.

Hamid, AbdulWahid (1995) *Islam, the Natural Way.* New Revised Edition 2007. Muslim Education and Literary Services. www.melspublications.com.

Lemu, B. Aisha (1996) *Islamic Aqidah and Fiqh: A textbook of Islamic belief and jurisprudence.* Chicago: IQRA' Educational Foundation.

Sarwar, Ghulam (2006) *Islam: Beliefs and Teachings.* 8th Edition. London: The Muslim Educational Trust.

DAILY SUPPLICATIONS

No Muslim's education would be complete without knowledge of at least some of the daily prayers and supplications used and taught by the beloved Prophet Muhammad ﷺ. D'Oyen and Kidwai's *What Should We Say?* presents a small collection of the most commonly recited supplications for a variety of everyday situations, for ages 7+. For older children and adults, refer to Inam Uddin's more extensive selection, *Reflection of Pearls*, also available as an audio CD set. Both books contain the original Arabic text, English translation, and transliteration as a guide to correct pronunciation.

D'Oyen, F. M. and Kidwai, A.R. (1999) *What Should We Say?* A selection of prayers for daily use. Markfield: The Islamic Foundation.

Inam Uddin, Abdurrahman Ibn Yusuf (2005) *Reflections of Pearls: a Concise and Comprehensive Collection of Authentic Invocations and Prayers*. Santa Barbara, California: White Thread Press.

Inam Uddin, Abdurrahman Ibn Yusuf (2005) *Reflections of Pearls: a Concise and Comprehensive Collection of Authentic Invocations and Prayers*. Narrated by Imam Tahir Anwar. Double audio CD set. Santa Barbara, California: White Thread Press.

Index